Into the Wind

WILD HORSES OF NORTH AMERICA

Into the Wind

WILD HORSES OF NORTH AMERICA

JAY F. KIRKPATRICK

PHOTOGRAPHY BY
MICHAEL H. FRANCIS

NorthWord
PRESS, INC
Minocqua, WI 54548

NorthWord Press, Inc.
P.O. Box 1360
Minocqua, WI 54548

Designed by Wayne C. Parmley
Calligraphy by Linda P. Hancock

Printed in China

For a free catalog describing NorthWord's line of nature books
and gifts, call 1-800-336-5666.

Library of Congress Cataloguing-in-Publication Data

Kirkpatrick, Jay F.
    Into the wind : wild horses of North America / by Jay F.
    Kirkpatrick ; photography by Michael H. Francis
        p. cm.
    ISBN 1-55971-426-3 : $35.00
    1. Wild horses—North America. I. Francis, Michael H.
    (Michael Harlowe), 1953-   . II Title.
    SF360.3.N7K57   1994
    599.72'5—dc20   94-20822
                                                  CIP

TABLE OF CONTENTS

AUTHOR'S DEDICATION

For my wife, Kathie, who, more than anyone else, made this book possible, and to the memory of Sebastian, the greatest of wild horses.

Michael H. Francis

AUTHOR'S ACKNOWLEDGMENTS

A life's labor rests on the shoulders of many and is never the work of a single person. Thus, I express my gratitude to the many persons listed here and still others who I shall undoubtedly forget. Chief among those to whom I owe thanks is my close friend and colleague, John W. Turner, Jr., who has, for over 20 years, both thrilled with me to the beauty and majesty of wild horses and suffered through the losses of animals we have loved. Others to whom I owe much include L. Taylor and G. Nunn of the Bureau of Land Management, R. Daigneault, J. Karish, B. Rogers, R. Rector, G. Olson, K. Zimmerman, J. Kumer, A. Turner, G. Bottitta, and L. Points of the National Park Service, R. Naugle and R. Keiper of Penn State University, B.L. Lasley, S.E. Shideler, I.K.M. Liu, and M. Bernoco, of University of California–Davis, A. Rutberg and J. Grandy, of the Humane Society of the United States, A. Perkins, and K. Allen.

Jay F. Kirkpatrick

PHOTOGRAPHER'S DEDICATION

Gary Leppart

To my wife, Victoria,

May your wild spirit never be tamed!

PHOTOGRAPHER'S ACKNOWLEDGMENTS

This current project has been one of my most enjoyable to date. Wild horses are such an indelible part of the American West, living symbols of romance, adventure, and freedom. Without looking at my photography, I can still see wild horses running toward me through the panoramic dust-filled sunsets of the arid West.

Many people deserve credit for helping me through this project.

First to thank on the list is my family: my wife, Victoria, and daughters Elizabeth and Emily. Hopefully the photos in this book will help remind them of our little outing when we went looking for, and found, wild horses in the Pryor Mountains of Montana.

To my parents, John and Derline Francis: I can only say thanks from the bottom of my heart for raising me to appreciate nature.

Thanks to my good friend Gary Leppart who actually introduced me to the Pryor Mountain wild horses, and who wore out his Bronco taking me up and down jeep trails this past year and a half.

I'd also like to express my gratitude to the following for their invaluable help: the Bureau of Land Management in Oregon, especially E. Ron Harding; the BLM in Rock Springs, Wyoming, especially Thor Stephenson, Vic McDarment, and Jack Steinbrech; the China Lake Naval Weapons Center, especially Dallas D. Allen; Assateague Island National Seashore, especially Grace Bottitta; the Calgary Zoo/Devonian Wildlife Conservation Center, especially Dwight Knapik. The wild horses have good friends in Josh and Denise Warbuton and Reverend Floyd Schwieger.

It's my pleasure to be able to share with you, the reader, a handful of the 9,000 plus photos I've taken in the past year and a half. Hopefully, between Dr. Kirkpatrick's text and my photography, you'll get a feeling for the special animals called wild horses and for the places we call wild horse country.

Michael H. Francis

FOREWORD

For millions of years ancestors of the modern horse roamed over wide plains, grazing on grasses and using their great speed to escape predators. A measure of their success is that they ranged in large numbers over great stretches of Europe and Asia. However, in the last million or so years, a new competitor arose that would greatly alter the lives of horses . . . a mammalian species relatively small in stature, without sharp claws or large teeth, known as man. Instead of using speed or strength as a weapon, this species used cunning. In a short time, geologically speaking, this new competitor had driven to extinction large, powerful animals like the mastodon and mammoth.

Fortunately, about 10,000 years ago, some particularly creative individual realized that instead of living a nomadic lifestyle, following wandering herds of ungulates in the hopes of harvesting enough meat for food, it would be wiser to tame some animal species in a process called domestication. For animals like cattle and sheep, this meant protecting them from predators and keeping them alive, at least for a while, to obtain supplies of milk and wool. However, man had other plans in mind for horses. Instead of using them for meat, milk, or for hides, man took advantage of their strength and speed.

Unlike cattle and sheep, which shared their lives with lowly shepherds and peasants, horses became the favorite animals of kings, queens, and soldiers. Horses pulled carts and chariots and carried riders with speed over wide stretches of the globe. They became so valuable that all the different kinds of horses living across Asia and Europe were captured and brought into captivity (although Przewalski's horse, the last remaining wild horse breed, apparently survived in remote areas of Asia into the mid-twentieth century.)

Yet, over the years, whenever horses could escape the chains of domestication, they took up living again in the wild. Jay Kirkpatrick's book, *Into the Wind*, celebrates these special populations. Like Jay, I prefer to think of these beautiful creatures as wild rather than as feral. Today in the western United States and in many other parts of the world as well, horses have proven to be so successful at reverting to lives in the wild that they have created controversy by outcompeting domestic livestock.

It is easy to measure the value of domestic horses, from the thoroughbreds that race at Churchill Downs to the Appaloosa carrying a handicapped child. But what about the value of wild horses? Are they "worth" anything? If they are, how can we help make sure they remain a part of the natural landscape of North America?

One thing for sure is that wild horses generate strong feelings, running on a continuum from strong hate on one end to strong love on the other. Survival of wild horse populations, however, depends less on emotion than on learning as much as possible about how wild horses live. Although they were an important part of both the Native American and frontier cultures of the western United States, wild horses were ignored by animal scientists until the early 1970s. But passage of the Wild Horse and Burro Act changed that. With support primarily from the Bureau of Land Management, graduate students began to study populations of wild horses for a year or two, write a master's thesis, then move on to study a "real" wildlife species. While these short-term studies provided

some insight, they only allowed small, isolated glimpses into the complex lives of wild horses.

What was needed was someone who loved wild horses and had the scientific know-how and the dedication to make studying them a long-term commitment. Dr. Jay Kirkpatrick is that unique individual. An Easterner by birth, Jay moved to Billings, Montana, shortly after completing a doctorate in reproductive physiology from Cornell University in 1971. The Pryor Mountain Wild Horse Refuge, southeast of Billings on the Montana-Wyoming border, provided an outdoor laboratory where he began to learn the behavior and social organization as well as the internal physiology of wild horses. Using the information gained in the Pryors, Jay tackled one of the major problems relating to wild horse survival—how to deal with wild horse fertility—and he came up with a creative solution. Rather than spending large sums of federal money to round up and then provide food for hundreds of horses waiting to be "adopted," Kirkpatrick proposed controlling wild horse populations by regulating reproduction.

Experimenting first with hormones to reduce sperm counts in stallions, Jay moved on to directing fertility control toward the mare. He developed a procedure for delivering a vaccine in the field that made mares immune to their own eggs, preventing pregnancy. The vaccine was more than 95 percent effective, and its effects were reversible. It didn't alter mare behavior or the basic social structure, it was relatively inexpensive to produce, and it didn't pass through the food chain.

Today Jay and his fertility control vaccine are in demand worldwide, for the technique appears adaptable to most mammalian species. Yet he still manages to find the time to visit old friends in the Pryors and wade through the broad marshes of Assateague Island, Maryland. When our paths cross there we spend time reminiscing about the blue-eyed stallion, Hot Air Balloon, and grieving still over the loss of the pinto, Sebastian, in a winter tidal surge. We celebrate the birth of yet another foal to T6 and the success of Smudge in harem-building.

Jay Kirkpatrick is a champion of wild horses. To their cause he has brought the cold eye of science and the warm heart of compassion. To him they have value simply because they are magnificent creatures that have survived all that nature and man has thrown at them. After you've read this book, I think you'll arrive at the same conclusion.

Dr. Ronald R. Keiper

Distinguished Professor of Biology–Penn State University

PREFACE

The small band of wild horses watched me intently from their grassy hideaway on the mountain slope above. Alert as deer, they quivered and stomped nervously, the herd stallion blowing loudly in an attempt to catch my scent. I froze in my downwind position, thrilled at my first sight of these wild Pryor Mountain horses and exhausted from the effort to find them.

I had discovered this day that finding these horses was much like looking for a moving needle in a haystack. The Bureau of Land Management had given me hints as to where the horses might be found, and I had set out into these remote south-central Montana mountains optimistically. Chattering along in my old green International Scout, I bounced cautiously through the semi-passable, washed out gullies known as mining roads. The mountains rose darkly from their near desert roots, and in the immensity of the desolate and lovely landscape, I began to wonder just how I would ever find the horses.

Parking the Scout, I eased into the hills of pine, stunted juniper, and mountain mahogany, using every hunting skill I had ever developed to sneak quietly along while looking for signs. Despite the coolness of a 60-degree autumn day, sweat ran down my brow as I struggled up the jumbled rock slopes. I stalked for hours beneath a perfect blue Montana sky, and when I was beginning to believe the horses were a myth, I discovered fresh tracks and droppings. I knew then that the horses must be near.

When I poked cautiously from a forested slope and saw the horses on the ridge above, it was obvious that they had long known of my approach. Torn between curiosity and fear, they paused to study me, and I was immediately struck by their wildness. In that unforgiving land these horses, so very different from any other horses I had ever seen, were utterly untamed. The thought of these horses, surviving in this forgotten place through toughness and intelligence, filled me with excitement.

Stocky and muscular, smaller than I had imagined, the horses came in every color. The stallion was black as night, his broad white face like a beacon. A buckskin mare with a dorsal stripe down her back and tiger-striped legs stood near a steel gray mare who shared her tiger striping. A strawberry roan mare with white face and three white stockings looked nervously in my direction, tossing her head. Prancing about was a sorrel foal of the year with a snip and two white socks. A stallion no more than two years old—and as black as the herd stallion that was likely his sire—turned toward me, his forehead ablaze with a perfect white star. All had full, long tails, longer than any I'd ever seen, and they stood achingly beautiful in the afternoon sun.

Flaring his nostrils, the herd stallion lifted his head and began blowing. A mare whinnied an answer. The tenseness of the herd grew palpable. Wheeling to the rear of the herd, the stallion whinnied explosively and in an instant was driving the horses up the slope before him. Rocks clattered and dust flew as they raced up the rocky ridge, topping the rise with ease and grace.

For one last time the stallion paused, looked my way, and whinnied. I held my anxious breath as he pitched away, driving his herd into the maze of canyons and coulees beyond, swallowed up by the Pryor Mountains.

Though I did not know much about wild horses that afternoon in 1971, I instinctively knew that I had just seen an extraordinary species of wildlife.

hen I first arrived in Montana in 1970, I was a young assistant professor fresh out of graduate school and looking for a way to put my training as a reproductive physiologist to work. It was Dr. John Craighead, the noted grizzly bear researcher, who suggested that I apply my training to problems of reproduction in wildlife species, a subject about which we knew very little. By chance, at the same time, the U.S. Congress was passing the Free Roaming Wild Horse and Burro Act, affording wild horses almost complete protection from destruction by humans. These two seemingly unrelated events conspired to send me on a 25-year journey into the heart of America's—and indeed the world's—wild horse country.

Two employees of the Bureau of Land Management (BLM), the agency that was charged with the management of the wild horses, foresaw the rapid increase in wild horse populations that would take place over the next decade and the need for publicly acceptable methods of controlling these animals. They visited me at my laboratory and asked, "Can you make horses stop reproducing?" In my naivete, I assured them I could. As it turned out, it took almost the entire 25 years to figure out how to do that, but along the way I was completely absorbed by this strange animal, the wild horse.

I immediately enlisted the help of my former classmate from graduate school, Dr. John Turner—by then at the Medical College of Ohio—and we set about to "save" America's wild horses. We first reviewed the available literature on the biology of the wild horse, which in 1972 consisted of only two unpublished papers. These provided only a bit of help; we were shocked to learn how little was known about wild horses. We would have to start from scratch.

Between 1972 and 1976, John, my wife, Kathie, and I combed the hills, gullies, forests, and sands of the Pryor Mountain National Wild Horse Refuge. We suffered the 130-degree heat of the summers and the minus 40-degree cold of winters, and we lived with the 130 or so horses that roamed this harsh but beautiful land. Today we refer to those times as the "grain bin" years, because we slept in a small government trailer that had been converted into a grain bin for domestic horses. At night our sleeping bags were literally covered with multitudes of scurrying mice.

During those four years, we had the delightful experience of coming face to face with one of North America's most beautiful and majestic wildlife species. We quickly learned about their complex social organization and the close and intricate social relationships between individuals. Over time I became familiar with individuals and watched and learned as they grew from foals to adults. I can still see the streaming tail and rippling muscles of powerful Citation, the black herd stallion. There was also Blue Floyd, the blue-roan stallion who met his end in 1979 on the horns of a bison. And there was Dahlia, the spooky black mare who over the years never relaxed for one moment. My favorite was smart and gentle Tiger Lily, the buckskin mare with the dark dorsal stripe and black tiger-striping. Even during the good months these animals eked out a living. During the agonizing blast furnace summers they spent hours pawing for water in the drying springs.

On the edge of Montana's Bighorn Canyon, three horses pause a moment
before disappearing into the arid desert country of their home range.

During the fiercely cold winters of 1977-78 and 1978-79, I watched nearly half die laboring in the four-foot snows. And, of all the knowledge I gained and the emotions I felt, nothing was as great as the respect I developed for these animals.

Between 1975 and 1977, observation gave way to hands-on experiences. If we were to develop contraceptives for wild horses, we first had to learn about their hormone concentrations, for which we needed blood samples. We captured Pryor horses by driving them into fenced enclosures. At first I was apprehensive about all this, but the care and skills of Lynne Taylor and Gene Nunn, two BLM wranglers who could make ropes talk, softened my concern. Not a single horse died and only a few suffered minor injuries. As we anxiously studied the samples, the very first picture of basic wild horse reproductive endocrinology was revealed. My respect for the animals grew.

The years passed. While the focus of my work with wild horses centered on fertility control, I expanded my study to learn more about their natural history. Where had these wild horses come from? Was the theory true that some wild horses were descendants of the original Spanish mustangs brought to this continent in the 1500s? How did wild horses subsist on the sparse vegetation of their desolate ranges, and how did they survive disease, cold, heat, and predators? Were wild horses inbred and, if so, what might be the effects upon them? By 1980, several other investigators around the United States and Canada had initiated their own studies with wild horses. Richard Miller and Lee Boyd studied the behavior of wild horses from the Red Desert of Wyoming, Ron Keiper was well along with his seminal studies of the Assateague Island wild horses, and Dan Rubenstein was adding to our knowledge of barrier island wild horses on the Shackleford Banks off the coast of North Carolina. Joel Berger was studying wild horses of the Great Basin and several other investigators were examining wild horse behavior in New Mexico, Colorado, Oregon, Alberta, and Sable Island. While these additional studies added to our basic knowledge of wild horses, they also spawned controversy.

One of the first surprises was that neither behavior nor reproductive success was the same across the many varied locations of the continent's wild horses. Horse bands with multiple stallions were almost unheard of in the Pryor Mountains or elsewhere, but almost half the bands of the Red Desert had more than one mature stallion.

Water is key to the survival of America's western wild horses, and the animals may have to travel miles on some ranges in order to quench their thirst. During dry seasons, some horses water only once a day or even less.

Wild mares in almost all herds went off by themselves to have their foals, but in the Red Desert they simply laid down and gave birth next to the band. Reproductive rates were very high in Nevada and relatively low on Assateague Island, and some horses on the Shackleford Banks displayed territorial behavior, something that no other wild horses have done. What could account for all this diversity in biology?

The answers were needed not merely to stem scientific curiosity but to better manage the herds. Management policies were emerging from government offices based on the biology of a single herd, policies that failed to reflect the diverse biology displayed by America's wild horses. Unfounded concerns about inbreeding led to attempts to dilute the bloodlines of unique populations. Policy-makers failed to understand basic horse biology, leading to programs that removed young animals from herds—which only resulted in increased reproduction by those horses that remained. By 1980 there were perhaps 70,000 wild horses on public lands in the United States, and still no publicly acceptable means of controlling the populations existed. What had seemed so simple at first became a political meat grinder.

By 1980, my work began to take me to new wild horse ranges. Near Susanville, I studied the rather large horses of northern California. On the Challis wild horse range of central Idaho we carried out field studies of our first method of stallion fertility control. I had to see for myself the horses of the Red Desert with their social behaviors that defied all convention. And I visited the little primitive wild horses of southeastern Oregon. At the invitation of the Australian government, I marveled near Alice Springs at some of the Northern Territory's 600,000 wild horses. Kathie and I wandered to the billabongs where the horses—"brumbies" as they know them "down under"—came to water. Wherever we journeyed in the outback we encountered a profusion of skeletons, the remains of the thousands of horses that die annually from the rigors of drought.

My work continued to grow more interesting. By 1986, all our efforts at horse contraception had been pharmacologically successful. That is, although we had developed wild horse contraceptives, we had yet to discover

a practical means of delivering it to a large number of horses. In 1986, the National Park Service invited us to Assateague Island to find a humane method to control these wonderful barrier island horses, which had lived there for 360 years. By this time, John Turner and I were joined by Irwin Liu, from the University of California–Davis, and we took a new approach to fertility control—immunocontraception. In the end we were successful with our research, but that is another story. The real magic of the Assateague experience was built around these magnificent animals and their life histories.

The previous 12 years of behavioral work and careful genealogy developed by Ron Keiper opened the door to one of the most novel and rewarding experiences I have had with wild horses. Suddenly I saw that the interaction of horses—these beautiful pintos, bays, and sorrels—was much more intricate than I'd imagined. I could see the relationships between horses: brothers and sisters, mothers and daughters, fathers and sons, even cousins and grandparents. Often the behavioral traits of a parent became apparent in the offspring. My respect grew, and out of this respect sprang a new sensitivity for the animals. We had to study how the mares' ovaries were functioning after contraception, we had to estimate fetal loss during the winter, and we had to diagnose pregnancy in animals that we were not allowed to handle. In collaboration with B. L. Lasley, the scientist who pioneered the use of urinary hormone analysis in zoo animals at the San Diego Zoo, we learned how to do the same thing with the wild horses of Assateague. Today, we can point to a half-dozen scientific advances in veterinary medicine, wildlife biology, and wildlife contraception that came directly from the Assateague wild horses. Perhaps equally important is that what we learn from today's wild horses provides insights of how evolution shaped the original wild horse.

As the twilight of my own career approaches, I feel very fortunate to have spent my professional life with these magnificent animals. Their future is still clouded and it will require an enlightened attitude by governmental agencies and vigilance by the public to ensure a proper and humane future for the wild horse. Perhaps in some way, this book will help to bring about a better understanding of America's wild horses.

AROUND THE WORLD IN 12,000 YEARS

A petroglyph from White Mountain, Wyoming, is a reminder of the close relationship between Indian horse cultures and the "Medicine Dog."

n an October day in 1519, somewhere near the site of present-day
Vera Cruz, a group of stallions, mares, and a foal born aboard ship on
the long voyage, stepped ashore on a beach on the east coast of what is today
Mexico. One can only imagine these horses, alert and unsettled after the boat trip
from the Caribbean, nervously pawing at the sand. Whinnying and snorting and
generally being uncooperative with their Spanish handlers, they probably looked to
one another for the comfort that horses find with others of their species. Among the 17
horses were chestnuts, grays, dark and light bays, a pinto, a sorrel, and a roan. After a few
moments of nervousness, the horses were led from the beach to the rocky soil of Mexico,
completing in those steps a 12,000-year, around-the-world odyssey. The species *Equus
caballus*, the modern horse, was home again in the land of its origin.

These unassuming animals belonged to Hernando Cortez and were part of an
expeditionary force that would ultimately conquer the Aztec Empire. As large as this historic event would become in the annals of human history, the reintroduction of the horse
to its native land loomed equally large in the saga of biological history. This unusual animal,
which had already played such a huge role in the history of man in Asia and Europe, was
now poised to do the same thing in North America. The 17 horses, of course, had no idea
of their Old World legacy nor of their future. They were probably concerned only with one
another and from where the next meal would come. The soils of North America would
tremble again under the hooves of the horse for the first time in over 10,000 years.

Technically, the horse was reintroduced to the New World in 1493. As part of
Columbus's second voyage, 25 horses—15 stallions and 10 brood mares—were landed
in the Caribbean. In 1514 the animals were brought to the shores of South America.
These were but brief previews to the coming of Cortez's horses, an event we generally
look upon as more profound. For it is the North American continent, and not the islands
of the Caribbean, on which fossil evidence paints the picture of the origin of the genus
Equus and its evolution to the species *caballus*, the modern horse.

The arrival of horses on the shores of Mexico nearly 500 years ago is but a blink
in the 60-million-year history of this species. However, their arrival is important if we are
to understand the complex nature of this animal and how we, their sometime friend, per-
ceive them. There will be those who, upon reading this book, will immediately object to
my reference to wild horses. Free-roaming horses, regardless of their location, are generally
considered to be feral—a domestic species that has lost its social relationship to man and
now fends for itself in the wild.

While technically correct, the feral designation falls far short of reflecting the
astounding abilities of a wild creature to wrest its living from deserts, mountains, prairies,
swampy estuaries, and barrier islands. It fails to project a picture of extremely wary animals,
most of which view man with the same affection they feel for mountain lions or bears. The
feral designation tends to create images of old barnyard plugs, standing on the edges of
farms and ranches, waiting for handouts or simply waiting to die because of their former

During the 1700s, wild horses roamed America's prairies in herds numbering in the millions.

(left) One of the most hostile environments for America's wild horses is the coastal barrier islands of the East Coast. Here, wild horses live in marshes and swamp lands year-round and must endure poor quality forage and large insect swarms. (below) Horses were first introduced to Assateague Island, off the coast of Maryland and Virginia, in the 1670s by English settlers who did not want to pay the king's taxes on fences.

owners' neglect. In the case of wild horses, nothing could be further from the truth. Thus, with no apologies to the purists, I shall refer, throughout this book, to the free-roaming horse of North America as wild.

Wild horses are also commonly referred to as exotics, animals that are biological strangers and that have been transported from their native habitats to foreign soil by the hand of man. Exotic species are thought of in mostly negative ways. The English sparrow, the starling, and the Norway rat are all exotics, brought here from Europe hundreds of years ago, and we have little in the way of tolerance for them. The feral pig is an excellent example of an exotic mammal. Placed in the wild throughout the world, the damage it inflicts on habitats has certainly fueled the negative connotations of the term exotic. On the other hand, we have exotics like the ring-necked pheasant, which was brought to North America for recreational purposes, that we value and protect. Thus the

term "exotic" carries with it all the biases of humans, for whom beauty—and ugliness—are always in the eyes of the beholder.

The wild horse may in fact be an exotic species in Australia, New Zealand, and a few other locations around the world, but it is certainly not so in North America. Horses evolved on this continent only to later disappear, possibly at the hand of man. After what can only be viewed as seconds on the hands of evolution's clock, the horse was returned by the same hand to resume its place among the same animals and plants with which it had evolved. To label the North American wild horse as an exotic ignores the facts of time and evolutionary history.

Thus, the wild horse differs from this continent's other large ungulates in that there is a lack of agreement that it is even a wild species. If this book has one most compelling theme, it is that there is truly a

Wild horses are at home in mountain habitats with elevations as high as 10,000 feet. Although the winters here can be harsh, often there is more water and grass in these locations.

North American wild horse, deserving of the same admiration and respect we give to the other species of the continent. My own bias, after 23 years of living with this remarkable creature on several continents, is that it probably deserves more admiration and respect. Remember, we humans made it here to North America only about 12,000 to 15,000 years ago. However, the horse began its round-the-world journey here in North America over 60 million years ago. Just which of us is the exotic species?

This journey was begun by *Hyracotherium*, a small rabbit-like beast thought to be the oldest direct ancestor of the horse. The earliest fossil records of the horse come from the Eocene epoch, about 50 to 60 million years ago. They provide us with a picture of *Eohippus* —the "Dawn Horse"—an animal perhaps 12 inches tall with four toes on the front legs and three on the hind legs. *Eohippus* is one of the horse's earliest known ancestors. Similar proto-horse fossil remains have been found throughout North America, Great Britain, and Europe. But only in North America did the race appear to survive long enough to advance to the next evolutionary step.

Rich fossil remains found throughout North America's Great Plains depict the next 35 or so million years. The evolutionary process sculpted and shaped the horses' forebears in a variety of ways, producing at least five major varieties. These new forms included, in chronological order: *Mesohippus* (30 million years), whose fossil remains are particularly rich in South Dakota and Colorado; *Miohippus* (25 million years); *Parahippus* (20 million years); and *Merychippus* (15 million years). Each new variety was a bit larger than the one before it, with toes of the feet progressively reduced in number or fused. They evolved the high-crowned teeth and larger muscles of mastication (chewing), which permitted these forerunners of the modern horse to shift from a diet of leaves to one of grasses. During the middle Pleistocene, about 7 to 10 million years ago, no less than eight recognized species of pre-equids evolved from *Merychippus*.

About 3 million years ago, during the Pliocene or Glacial Epoch, the species *Pliohippus* is thought to have given rise to several species and to the emergence of the genus *Equus* (meaning large). One of these species, *Equus simplicidens*, may have been the earliest member of *Equus*. Fossil remains of *E. simplicidens* have been found in Idaho, in rock about 3.3 millions years old. *Equus* possessed only a single toe, which today we recognize as a hoof.

It is this peculiarity, the odd number of toes, that places the horse—along with all other members of *Equidae*—in the order *Perissodactyla*. Horses share this feature with the rhinoceroses of the Old World and the tapirs of both South America and Southeast Asia. It also distinguishes them from the *Artiodactyla*, or even-toed ungulates, such as deer, cattle, antelope, and many other well-known hoofed species.

The fossil remains of early *Equus* bear great similarity to the living equid species of today and were found from as far south as Texas to as far north as Alaska and east to Kansas—and included animals described as horses, asses, and even zebras. In North America, this forerunner of the modern horse was apparently a highly successful mammal throughout the Pleistocene. On the basis of fossil remains from Arizona, several scientists have claimed that early *Equus* was more abundant than the bison and second in numbers

Przewalski's horse, or the Mongolian wild horse, is thought to be the progenitor of today's horses. It is characterized by a stocky body, a brush-cut mane, an aggressive disposition, and two more chromosomes than the modern horse. This horse could have been the model for hundreds of prehistory cave paintings in Europe and Asia.

only to the mammoth. It is important to remember that the earliest of the equids was already a very successful group of species, a characteristic that would carry one of its descendants—the modern horse—to success again, in modern times, around the world.

At some point in evolutionary history, several variations of the evolving equids resembling *E. simplicidens* found their way to Eurasia, presumably by migrating across the Bering land bridge into Asia. There is no fossil evidence thus far to indicate *Equus* evolved anywhere but in North America. The true horse, or caballoid horse, emerged from the genus *Equus* in North America about 2 million years ago and resembled the Przewalski's horse of today. Just as it is clear that the genus *Equus* originated in North America rather than in Eurasia, the true horse also originated in North America, and the numerous migrations back and forth across the Bering land bridge included both early equids and caballoid horses. At least one point in time after their dispersal to Eurasia the genus *Equus* disappeared from North America for a long period of time—perhaps 100,000 years. Then, perhaps 500,000 to 600,000 years ago they returned to North America, undoubtedly by the same route they left. While the evolution of the horse then continued on in North America, those earlier migrations to Asia would turn out to be the events that later spared the horse from eventual extinction.

Nothing in nature is constant. The phenomenally successful North American biological history of the horse came to a mysterious and relatively abrupt end about 12,000 years ago. The species that had been so successful during two separate epochs of evolutionary time simply vanished from the continent, as did a few other grazing species, like the camel and the mammoth. But most, like the bison and antelope, not only survived, they flourished.

The causes given for the extinction of the horse in North America are of course all speculative. Changing climate can hardly be blamed in light of the survival of less adaptable animals, like the antelope, and a change in food is also unlikely, considering the survival of the bison. Perhaps a species-specific disease spread among the horses, but no strong evidence exists to support that idea either. The most widely accepted idea today is that man had a hand in the matter. The one epochal event that coincided with the disappearance of the horse from North America was the arrival of man. It has been suggested by several scientists that Paleolithic man simply hunted the horses into extinction, along with several other large species (for example, the mammoth) within the time span of only a few thousand years. Whatever the causes, the sound of the horses' pounding hooves would not to be heard in North America for another 10,000 to 12,000 years.

To understand the remarkable history of our modern wild horse, we must now return to Asia several million years ago, to where early variants of the evolving horse had migrated. It is well beyond the scope of this book to follow the detailed speculation of just how the modern horse evolved in Asia, but two theories that I will encapsulate here are important if we are to understand and appreciate the wild horses of today's world.

On the steppes of northeastern China and Mongolia evolved a short, stocky, dun-colored horse with an upright, zebra-type mane that was first described in 1881. Sometime during the latter part of the nineteenth century, one of these horses was killed by Kirgiz tribesmen of the Gobi Desert. By good fortune, the explorer N. M. Przewalsky obtained the skull and hide of this animal and passed them along to I. S. Poliakov, of the Zoological Museum of St. Petersburg. Poliakov in turn classified the animal as a new species of *Equidae* and named it *Equus przewalskii*—the Przewalski's horse, more commonly known as the Mongolian wild horse. Seventeen years passed before the first live Przewalski's horse was captured in 1898. By the early part of this century the species was thought to be extinct in the wild, largely at the hands of Mongolian herdsmen who shot the animals because they believed the horse competed with their livestock for limited water and grass. Fortunately a large population of Przewalski's horses had already been captured. Breeding programs in the world's zoos have brought the numbers from 206 in 1973 to more than 1,000 in 1993, and plans are underway to reintroduce and reestablish a population in the animals' native Mongolia. Technically, the Przewalski's horse is the world's only true wild horse, my own biases notwithstanding, even though it does not yet exist in the wild.

While the modern horse has 64 chromosomes, Przewalski's horse has 66. One theory is that over the course of time, four of the chromosomes of the Przewalski horses became just two, in a process known as Robertsonian translocation. If true, this event resulted in the emergence of *Equus caballus*, the modern horse.

Another recent ancestor of the modern horse was known to exist in the Pleistocene epoch. The tarpan was a small gray horse, with upright mane and dorsal stripe, that inhabited the lowlands of Europe. But it was driven to extinction by 1851, when the last known tarpon was killed in the Ukraine. We have no genetic evidence for the number of its chromosomes, and speculation abounds about whether the tarpan evolved directly from *Equus przewalskii*. It is noteworthy that 15,000-year-old late Pleistocene horse fossils from New Mexico show bone structure extremely similar to that of *Equus przewalskii*. Whatever the truth may be, these two species are at the roots of the modern horse's family tree. While the tarpan

Wild horses in Theodore Roosevelt National Park's South Unit are at home in the rugged badlands of the Dakotas. Except for winter blizzards, these badlands make a good habitat for wild horses because of the plentiful grass and water.

no longer exists, those interested in the origins of wild horses should take the opportunity to view captive Mongolian wild horses. Therein lies the genetic background for one of the world's most successful species.

Regardless of the origin of *Equus caballus*, the modern horse found its place in human history. Up until about 4300 B.C., all the world's horses were wild. The largest populations lived upon vast grasslands, from the Ukraine west to Mongolia, with smaller populations of horses in Europe. Archaeological evidence indicates that horses were then a part of the human diet. The earliest evidence for the horse's domestication comes from 6,000-year-old Bronze Age cave drawings found near Kammenaya Mogila, Ukraine, that depict men on horseback. Supporting evidence of domestication comes from horse skeletons from this time period and location that reveal tooth wear that could only have occurred from mouth bits.

Men on horseback spread rapidly east from the Ukraine to the Asian steppes. By 1500 B.C. the horse carried Egyptians upon its back, and there is historical evidence for domestication in China by 1300 B.C. By 1000 B.C. the horse was a common domestic animal in Europe. After this landmark event of the horse's domestication, the issue of the origin of the modern horse from either tarpans or Przewalski's horses became moot. By the time of Christ, Chinese horses with probable *Equus przewalskii* origins were being exchanged regularly with stock from the Middle East and Europe, horses whose origin could be argued to be the tarpan. After this point in history, it is likely that genetically pure tarpans or Przewalski horses were doomed to extinction.

Before the horse found its way back home to North America, it had to undergo a great deal of selective breeding, and here the story of the horse becomes even more complicated and controversial. One of the oldest breeds (not species) of horse is the Arabian, and another closely related breed is the African barb. The former was the domesticated form of the horse that found its way across the Middle East. As a breed it is thought to be at least 200,000 years old. It is thought to have evolved directly from some sort of caballoid horse that also gave rise to Przewalski's horse. The African barb emerged along the Barbary coast of North Africa. Great and spirited controversy surrounds which came first—the Arabian or the barb—a subject that we will not pursue here. Both breeds were on the small side, as modern domestic breeds go, and were characterized by good speed and high levels of endurance, qualities that appealed to soldiers. However, the small size was a disadvantage because soldiers of the time were armored and weighed a great deal.

At the same time, soldiers of northern Europe found themselves with the opposite problem. There, they had what some historians refer to as the Norse horse, a large animal of the European forests that resembled today's draft horse. It could certainly carry armored knights, but it lacked the speed and the toughness of its smaller Middle Eastern and African cousins. What armies needed was a horse with the speed, toughness, and endurance of the Arabian and barb—but with the size to bear the weight of the armored knight. To accomplish this goal, horse breeders of the time turned to genetic engineering, albeit a more primitive form than we read about today. By selectively breeding the Norse horse with barbs, they brought together all the qualities requisite for good war horses. The principal location for this experiment in selective breeding was the Spanish province of Andalusia, and hence the origin of the Andalusian horse, the breed that Columbus and early Spanish explorers brought to the New World. With that journey, these horses closed the circle of time and distance to set hoof again upon the shores of their evolutionary origin.

During the 50 years following Columbus's introduction of Andalusians onto islands of the Caribbean, the need for horses by the Spanish explorers exceeded the ability to transport animals from Spain. Horse breeding operations were established in these tropical islands, but these too failed to meet the demand. Soon large numbers of pure barbs were being transported to the New World. To be sure, the wild horses of North America are far more genetically diverse than these first pioneering equids of the 1500s, but the blood of their Spanish relatives may still course through the veins of a small number of wild horses today.

It would be a mistake to assume that the earliest genetic contributions to our present-day wild horses came only from the horses of the early Spaniards. As early as 1565, shipwrecked horses found their way onto the shores of the Shackleford Banks (otherwise known as Shackleford Island). In 1670, English settlers inhabiting present-day Maryland and Virginia placed horses on Assateague Island, a coastal barrier island on the Atlantic coast. The King had placed a tax on colonial fences, and the settlers found it easier, and cheaper, to simply turn horses loose on the island and let the waters of the Atlantic Ocean and Chincoteague and Sinepuxent bays keep the horses from wandering off. History tells us that later, in 1820, the Spanish ship San Lorenz ran aground on shoals off the coast of Assateague—and that among its cargo were horses. Popular legend has it that an undetermined number of an undetermined breed of horse survived the wreck, swam ashore, and mixed with the original English horses. No one knows for sure whether there is truth in that legend. It is a romantic story that one would like to be true.

Whatever their genetic origins—there were many, to be sure—and regardless of where the horses were introduced in North America, they soon found freedom, either by purposeful release by their owners or by escape. They spread across the land with unprecedented speed and success. In the West, horses found their way into the Great Basin and spread as far north as present-day Oregon and Idaho. To the east of the Rocky Mountains, the horses spread out from lands that are now New Mexico and Texas, north and east across the Great Plains, reaching the Canadian border by the early 1600s. Horses released or escaped in the area of present-day Florida moved north and west and up the Mississippi Valley. By the 1700s, the horse population of the Great Plains had grown to staggering numbers. Although no one can provide evidence for accurate numbers, most scholars of the subject agree that wild horses numbered in the millions. Whatever the true count, only bison outnumbered the wild horse.

If the story of the genetic origin of the North American wild horse ended here, we could permit ourselves to subscribe to the romantic notion that today's wild herds are the descendants of the original Spanish Andalusians and barbs. However, the eighteenth century brought the English, French, and American trappers west, riding upon every imaginable breed of horse. Many of these escaped and joined the wild herds. Sometimes the trapper simply succumbed to the elements and the horses were on their own. In other cases, Indians stole the trapper's horses, adding these to their own herds. The Indian herds in turn were raided by wild stallions looking for mares, further adding to the diversity of the wild herds. In the nineteenth century, miners, farmers, and cattlemen brought more horses, representing more breeds, which added again to the genetic melting pot.

The final great infusion of blood into North America's wild horse herds came with the Great Depression. Imagine, if you will, thousands of small farms and ranches across the great expanses of the western plains and the Great Basin. Crops failed, markets collapsed, and people quietly packed up and moved on, leaving behind shattered dreams, decaying buildings, and of course, their livestock. Among the latter were horses. While most other large farm animals soon succumbed to the elements, the horses followed a recurring theme: they survived to join their wild relatives. The stage was now set for their greatest test of all, one that they had apparently fought and lost 12,000 years before—surviving the presence of man.

The history of the North American wild horse would be incomplete without at least a passing mention of the horse's influence upon the Native American Indian. This story is profound, and the effects of horses upon the continent's native peoples are unprecedented in anthropological history. The first Indians of the continent to see the horse were the Aztecs of Mexico and, soon thereafter, the tribes of the southwestern United States. Not only were they seeing horses for the first time, they were seeing men on horses. Their reactions were hardly surprising. What they saw were not men sitting upon animals, but instead centaur-like creatures—men growing from the bodies of horses. If that was not frightening enough for the Indians, the bodies of these man-beast creatures could come apart, go their separate ways, and then rejoin later. The horse became god-like in the eyes of the Indian, and it was known as the medicine dog.

Few reliable sources tell when in history the Indian realized horses were not man-beast combinations. But we do know that as the Spanish domestic horse found its freedom and reverted to the wild, the Indians viewed them in a new and very natural light. According to Robert Denhard (*The Horse of the Americas*, University of Oklahoma Press) the earliest horses became a source of food. This should hardly be surprising when we view prehistoric man's relationship with the horse. It was a food source then, too, and many prehistoric European campsites are littered with the bones of horses. In any case, many of the first wild horses of the North American continent soon found themselves being roasted rather than ridden.

The precise point at which Indians gave up eating horses and began riding them is also obscure. We know that Indians were employed by the Spanish to care for the horses in the vicinity of what is now Santa Fe, New Mexico. It is thought that some learned to ride so

they could herd the Spaniard's cattle. If so, some surely shared their newfound knowledge with their own society. Whatever the truth, Indians were soon aboard *Equus caballus*, riding off into one of the most complete and rapid anthropological changes in history. By 1639 Southwestern Indians, probably Navajos and Apaches, were raiding the Spanish ranches for horses. In 1680 the Pueblo people revolted to drive the Spanish invaders from the region. The Spanish left behind thousands of horses, many of which found their way east into Texas.

Journals from various explorers document the progressive migration of horses north over the Great Plains, one of the two great pathways that horses would find, to reach Pawnee villages in Kansas by 1724. By 1796 the Sioux had exchanged their Minnesota canoes for horses and were already moving west across the Dakotas.

The second great northerly expansion of the horse occurred more rapidly up a pathway west of the Rockies. The Shoshone of Idaho were on horseback by about 1700, the Flathead of western Montana had horses by 1720, and likewise the Blackfoot of northern Montana just a few years later. This scenario is corroborated by eastern Montana's Crow Indians, whose legends credit the Nez Perce, of Idaho, with introducing them to horses from west of the Continental Divide. The likely route for the Great Basin expansion of the horse started at Santa Fe, spread up the Colorado River, along the Snake, and up the Green River. Lewis and Clark reported seeing hundreds of wild horses along the Columbia River valley in 1804.

The Indians had no tradition of horsemanship, but they improvised and learned fast. While the white men brutalized themselves and young horses to break them for riding, the Indian learned to lead unbroken horses into shoulder-deep water, climb aboard, and let the horses exhaust themselves thrashing about in the stream. Instead of heavy leather saddles and tack, the Indians simply threw a blanket across the animal's back, and put a horsehair rope around the horse's jaw. They became expert riders—some have described the Plains Indians of the nineteenth century as the greatest light horse cavalry in the world. This amazing transformation occurred in less than 300 years.

The horse caused tremendous cultural changes among the Native Americans. Prior to the reintroduction of the horse onto the continent, Indians of the Great Plains lived near the river bottoms and in the woodlands on the eastern edge of the prairies. They had no easy way to cross the seas of grass or hunt the bison with success. The pre-horse Indian was anchored to those locations where food and shelter offered themselves to men on foot. The horse changed all that.

The tribes of the Great Plains rode out onto the prairies, carried their belongings with them on the backs of horses, and hunted the bison with deadly effectiveness. They became nomadic. The Sioux left the woodlands of Minnesota and became the lords and masters of the Dakotas. The Shoshone climbed out of their caves in the Rockies and emerged as rulers of the Wyoming high plains. The Comanche left their riverside dwellings and swept across the Staked Plains of western Texas, a land previously virtually uninhabited. The Nez Perce of Idaho and Washington used the horse to migrate annually to hunt the bison and replenish their wealth 400 to 500 miles to the east. Stories are similar throughout the range of the wild horse in the western United States. The horse became the single greatest mark of wealth among the native peoples. And the influence of the Indian upon the genetic wealth of the continent's wild horses was no less profound. Horses were traded, stolen (by other Indians and wild stallions alike), and moved about in large numbers—and with each transaction, planned or unplanned, the genetic diversity of the continent's wild horses became even greater.

Thus did the wild horse of North America come to be. If we are to view this animal as truly a wild species, and if we are to understand its natural history, then we must also take lessons from its relatives. There are seven extant, or living, species among the *Equidae*. These include two species that we have already discussed, *Equus caballus*, the modern horse, and *Equus przewalskii*, the Przewalski's horse, which for the moment is extinct in the wild.

A third species is *Equus asinus*, the wild ass. This species originated in North Africa and today consists of two recognized subspecies: the Somali and the Nubian wild ass. The domestic donkey is thought to have originated from the latter subspecies about 3400 B.C. in Mesopotamia. Like so many wild equids, this species is rare in the wild. To make matters more confusing, no one is sure just how much interbreeding has taken place between the two subspecies. It is doubtful that pure Nubian asses still exist, largely because of interbreeding with domestic donkeys.

(below) The well-known Assateague Island "ponies" are actually small horses. Pony is used to designate horses smaller than 14 hands, but there are genetic distinctions between real ponies and horses, even though they are the same species. This two-year-old Assateague horse greets its mother with a show of affection. (right) The range of habitats in which horses live and thrive is truly surprising. Here, a stallion stands among Joshua trees in a southern California desert, enduring sweltering heat without much drinking water.

Only about 400 Somali wild asses still inhabit eastern Ethiopia and a small population exists in zoos around the world.

One of the most interesting members of Equidae is *Equus hemionus*, or the Asiatic wild ass. Subspecies include the onager, of the Middle East; the kiang, native to Tibet; the kulan, of Mongolia; and the Indian wild ass. The onager was domesticated by the Sumerians of Mesopotamia. Stone carvings from about 2500 B.C. show these animals pulling chariots. Once again, *Equus hemionus* is rare across most of its native habitat.

The zebras make up the remaining three species of equids. Grevyi's zebra (*Equus grevyi*) is the rarest of the three zebra species and its survival in the wild is questionable. It is distinguishable by the many very narrow stripes—perhaps as many as 15—across its side, and by its large ears. Its native range extended from Somaliland north to Kenya. The common plains zebra (*Equus burchelli*) ranges from South Africa to Kenya. Recognized subspecies of the common zebra include Burchell's zebra, Grant's zebra, and Chapman's zebra. All are characterized by a few (five or six) broad stripes across their sides. This species is very common, and perhaps 300,000 still roam throughout east and central Africa. The seventh living species of the Equidae is *Equus zebra*, or the mountain zebra. This too is a rare species and is now restricted to the very southwest corner of Africa. It was nearly hunted to extinction around the turn of the century, but several small populations were saved by South African farmers, and today several hundred remain. Hartmann's zebra is a subspecies, with perhaps 6,000 animals surviving in the wild. Both subspecies can be distinguished from the other zebras by the number of stripes (from 10 to 12) across their sides—this falls somewhere between *E. grevyi* and *E. burchelli*. An eighth species, the Quagga (*Equus quagga*) existed into the early twentieth century. It lived exclusively in South Africa and was hunted into extinction. This species had striping only on the front half of its body and, interestingly enough, was the only species of zebra to be easily domesticated. Of the seven extant species of equids, most authorities consider only six to be wild species. *Equus caballus*, the modern horse, is not considered by these authorities to be wild, despite the fact that more of this one species of equid lives in the wild than any other, across a range spanning no less than six continents.

Finally, a word or two about the distinction between ponies and horses might be helpful, since we find both among wild populations in North America and around the world. Examples include the wild ponies of Exmoor, England, or the Pryor Mountain wild horses of Montana. Both horses and ponies belong to the same species, *Equus caballus*, and they really represent breeds of horse rather than subspecies. They can interbreed, but in truth there are some interesting physiological differences, particularly with regard to reproduction. Further complicating this issue is the fact that the terms pony and horse are often used to reflect size rather than breed. Any horse that stands less than 14 hands (56 inches) at the withers will be referred to as a pony, while those animals 14 hands or taller are horses. The well-known wild ponies of Assateague, for example, are in reality small horses and not ponies at all, while the Exmoor ponies of England are, in fact, genetic ponies. Confusion also arises from the claims that certain old breeds, such as barbs and tarpans, have been "reconstructed" through selective breeding. These claims are based only on the appearance and physical conformation of the horses in question but must be dismissed on scientific grounds. For example, the last tarpan was destroyed in 1851, and we have no way of even knowing how many chromosomes these animals had, let alone what other unique physiological characteristics they possessed. Extinction of subspecies and breeds is as real as extinction of species, and it is truly forever.

The wild horse is a novel creature. Although the horse was truly wild during prehistoric times, there are no records of the species' natural history. We have few clues about how it lived. Now that it is wild again, we must draw upon the biology of its closest living relatives if we are to understand and interpret what we see. Behavior, reproduction, social organization, and even physiology are all end products of the evolutionary process. We stopped that process in the modern horse several thousand years ago and bent the biology of this species to man's needs. Most of what we needed from horses, such as agreeable behavior, speed, size, color, markings, conformation, and so forth are of little value to what horses need and require.

We now have the opportunity to view the horse as a wild creature again, one responding to the forces of nature and natural selection. From these recent additions to our wildlife populations, we will learn the secrets of the original wild horses. For that reason alone they are a valuable resource. But for those who also appreciate beauty, and perhaps tenacity, and surely those who honor intelligence, the wild horse deserves and has earned its place among the world's wildlife.

THE HORSE AS
A SUCCESSFUL SPECIES

*S*lash was a resourceful pinto stallion with long white slashes down his side,
reminiscent of sea gull droppings. Wary and secretive, Slash and his mares
were archetypal barrier island wild horses. Wet, cool winters found this band, hidden and
suspicious of people, deep in the remote damp and grassy marshes of central Assateague Island.

But with the coming of summer and the hordes of insects it brought, Slash led his
band five miles north with unerring accuracy to the island's state park. Some may think that
these horses ventured this distance for human companionship and the possibility of hand-
outs—Slash once pursued a vacationer into his camper while trying to grab the man's box of Cheezits—but their real reasons
were much more practical and subtle. They came to take advantage of the park's lack of biting insects, which were held at bay
by campground managers who regularly fogged the area with insecticide.

There is little fresh water on Assateague. Normally, Slash would lead his band to drink from the saline, marshy back
bays. But to do so meant leaving the insect-free sands of the park and enduring the marsh's hordes of insects and flies. So, with
incredible resourcefulness, Slash learned to stand patiently near the campground's water spigot, waiting sometimes for hours for
a camper to wander by. When one did, Slash would stomp with a front hoof. Not everyone caught the horse's intentions, but
eventually someone at least as smart as Slash would come along and turn on the water.

As if to thank the camper, Slash would reward his trainee with an amazing array of facial expressions signifying his
satisfaction, then drink his fill of sweet, fresh water.

Wild though he was, Slash was also intelligent enough to take advantage of civilization's amenities.

e have taken a quick look at the history of the wild horse and now understand its almost exclusive status among the world's wildlife: a species that became extinct in the wild shortly after its domestication, only to reemerge as a wild species. This is no small task in a world in which survival for most wildlife has become more and more difficult. How has the horse managed to do this, against all odds? The answer lies in one of the wild horse's most important characteristics—its amazing adaptability. This adaptability allows wild horses to live under a great variety of climatic conditions, survive in diverse habitats, utilize a wide array of energy sources, and protect themselves from predators. Few species of large mammal have done all this as well as the horse.

Let us first consider the diverse habitats and climates in which wild horses have made themselves at home. Horses, as well as other equids, are primarily adapted to desert or semi-arid habitat, and that is in fact where most of the world's wild horses are found. But significant populations are also found high in the mountains, on unprotected steppes and plains, grassy islands in the North Atlantic, and marshes in estuaries in Europe. Almost no other large mammalian species has done as well in such diverse habitats.

The wild horses' adaptability does not surprise, considering the natural history of the other six species of wild equids. Although it no longer roams its native ranges, the Przewalski's horse lived upon the windswept steppes of Mongolia and western China. Water was scarce and temperatures were extreme, although high-quality grasses were abundant. The kiang, a wild ass inhabiting the highest valleys of Tibet, thrived at altitudes of 12,000 to 15,000 feet, enduring frigid temperatures, deep snows, and high winds of the mountain passes. At the other extreme, the Somali wild asses of the Danakil depression live close to 200 feet below sea level, with arid, furnacelike conditions. The common zebra dwells in a full range of habitats and precipitation extremes, from grassy savannas in East Africa to the very edges of the Kalahari Desert. Thus, the genetic seeds of adaptability are shared with the wild horse's remarkable relatives. Today's wild horses have reawakened these genetic assets to survive in a wide range of harsh environments.

Most North American wild horses have found homes in the deserts of Nevada, northeastern California, southeast Oregon, western Utah, western Colorado, and southern Wyoming. Little precipitation falls in these regions of sparse vegetation and water, where temperatures range from sweltering 100-degree highs to well below zero. Some populations of wild horses live in high mountain meadows at elevations of 9,000 feet near Challis, Idaho; on Montana's Pryor Mountain National Wild Horse Range, and in the Montgomery Pass Wild Horse Territory, straddling the California-Nevada border. Pryor Mountain wild horses are subjected to deep snows and extremely low temperatures. On several occasions I have observed these animals standing stoically for hours at a time in knee-deep snows and at temperatures lower than 30 degrees below zero. When it is time to feed, they move to windswept ridges where grasses remain exposed.

Most of the Great Plains have been given over to domestic livestock, but wild horses still inhabit the Badlands of Theodore Roosevelt National Park in North Dakota,

Today's wild horses provide clues to the evolutionary history of the horse.
It is clear that these animals have adapted to dry savannah and desert lands.

America's wild horses survive only where man has no use for the land or where refuges provide protection. Domestic livestock have replaced the great wild horse herds of an earlier time.

Wild horses are found as far north as Canada, and those living in northern latitudes or high mountains must endure subzero temperatures and driving blizzards. Only the strongest survive.

where not only are the temperatures extreme, but arctic winds sweep down across the prairies with unopposed fury. If those extremes are not impressive enough, North America's wild horses also live on a variety of islands off the east coast of the continent. One population, which arrived in the mid-1700s, lives on Sable Island in the middle of the North Atlantic, one hundred miles off the coast of Nova Scotia. Sable Island is characterized by sand dunes and beach grasses. Further south off the coasts of Maryland and Virginia, the famed horses of Assateague Island live in salt marshes for most of the year, enduring frequent northeastern storms that drive before them frigid winds and rain—and even hurricanes. To make matters worse, the horses must survive on low-quality marsh grass forage, have virtually no fresh water, and face insect numbers that stagger the imagination. The more southerly coastal islands farther off the Shackleford Banks and Carrot Island, in North Carolina, and Cumberland Island, off the coast of Georgia, provide gentler temperatures but no fewer hurricanes, tropical storms, and insects.

This remarkable adaptability of wild horses, and their amazing ability to survive and thrive in harsh environments, is something for which they can "thank" mankind. It is not by their choice that wild horses are found in such inhospitable environments. They are not stupid animals and would much prefer more hospitable environments, with abundant rich grasses, shelter from the extremes of weather, and plentiful and sweet water. One of the most dramatic examples of the wild horse's adaptability is found among the estimated 600,000 wild horses in the Northern Territories of Australia. During the wet years—if there is such a thing in central Australia—they thrive, reproduce, and live generally happy lives. When droughts come, the horses die by the thousands—perhaps by the hundreds of thousands. The outback near Alice Springs is littered with the remains of generations of these wild creatures. When the misery of drought ends and the grass grows once gain, those horses that have endured quickly repopulate the region. Wild horses around the world live where they do, not by choice, but because that is where they have been pushed by man. In these almost forgotten and forbidden corners of the world, places where man had little to gain, places that we considered useless for our own needs, wild horses have carved their niche.

(left) The Assateague mare "Cutthroat" provides an interesting picture of a feral animal eating a feral plant. The horses were not native to the coastal barrier islands, but neither were the reed-like phragmites, upon which this mare feasts. (below) Assateague horses can even thrive in the loblolly pine jungles of the island. "M17E" will consume greenbrier, thorns and all, and even poison ivy vines and leaves. This particular stallion of a roan-colored strain, is one of the few remaining animals on the island.

In addition to developing an ability to live in diverse climates, a successful wildlife species must be able to use diverse energy sources. Species that rely upon a single or small number of energy sources are vulnerable. With no chance of expanding its range, such species are often faced with extinction if too much pressure is placed upon its habitat. The giant panda's reliance upon flowering bamboo is a good example of a lack of adaptability. When the bamboo crop fails the pandas are in serious trouble. The wild horse, on the other hand, can utilize a wide variety of foods.

When food is varied and plentiful, wild horses selectively forage on grasses. Fossil evidence indicates that the earliest horses browsed primarily upon leaves and tender buds, much as do white-tailed deer. The change to high-crowned teeth that allow horses to graze efficiently on grasses was one of their most striking evolutionary steps. Wild horses of the western United States prefer wheatgrass, needlegrass, Indian ricegrass, and brome. When these are not available in sufficient quantities, they will eat sedges and a low, ground-dwelling, high-protein plant known as winterfat. But as even these food sources begin to dwindle, horses will turn to shrubs and even small trees. In the Pryor Mountains of Montana, I have witnessed wild horses consume bark and wood by gnawing two-inch-diameter mountain mahogany branches. If pressed sufficiently by the rigors of winter, they can be forced to subsist on Utah juniper, saltbush, greasewood, rabbitbrush, horsebrush, and big sagebrush, all wiry rough brush with little appeal to horses that have access to grasses. Faced with starvation and death, the wild horse will resort to browsing.

Protein content is extremely important in the diet of the wild horse, and it generally declines with the coming of winter. On the Red Desert of Wyoming, summer diets average 7.5 % crude protein and decline to 6% in the winter. In eastern Nevada I witnessed large numbers of wild horses in poor condition struggle through a bitter cold December. During the hot summers they live mainly upon grasses with crude protein contents of 3% to 5%. By December they were largely subsisting on winterfat, which though scarce in quantity has a protein content of over 8%. Thus, it appears that the wild horses of Nevada regulate their seasonal protein intake by eating large quantities of available low-protein grasses in the summer and small quantities of high-protein winterfat in the winter.

On coastal barrier islands, the diet of the wild horse is nothing short of astonishing. On Assateague Island, the primary food consists of several salt-marsh grasses. Left to themselves, the horses would spend their entire year on the tidal marshes along the bay. Even during the harshest of winters there is no shortage of these grasses. With the coming of warm weather, the dreaded mosquitoes and green-head flies emerge, driving the tortured horses from the grasses of their bay-side homes into the loblolly pine forests. While in the junglelike loblolly forests, the horses will amazingly consume great quantities of greenbrier, a vine-like plant that can best be described as a green barbed wire. This plant can rip boots and clothes to shreds, but the horses eat it! As spring and summer progress, the horses begin eating poison ivy in impressive quantities—leaves, vines, and all. They also eat the tender shoots of new-growth phragmites, a feral plant that resembles bamboo and that has invaded most East Coast barrier islands. I have often thought of the irony of a feral animal species eating feral plant species. After the insects become intolerable, the horses move to the windswept sand dunes in search of relief, where they eat American beach grass and browse on the tender branches of bayberry. Finally, as their retreat from the biting insects ends at the sea, the horses turn to living on dune grass. The ability to switch diets as conditions dictate, which most other wild ungulates do not have, provides horses with a tremendous advantage.

The horse's great latitude in selecting foods may be an adaptive behavior driven by a relatively inefficient digestive system. Horses are monogastric and have only a single stomach instead of the four that ruminants (cows, for example) possess. Because much of their food passes through their intestinal tracts without complete digestion, horses absorb fewer nutrients, increasing the need to be flexible in securing a variety of food.

This relatively ineffective single stomach has forced other adaptations in wild horses. Horses can consume their own feces to extract previously undigested, unabsorbed

nutrients. Although this is not a common habit for wild horses, several scientists, myself among them, have documented this behavior. Foals seem to practice this behavior most often, and it has been suggested that in this manner young horses acquire some of the bacteria necessary for digestion. Both mature and immature mares have also been witnessed eating from the large accumulations of aged and dried feces, known as stud piles, of stallions. This behavior has only been witnessed when winter weather has set in and food becomes scarce. The importance of this behavior in surviving long hard winters is not understood, but the behavior certainly gives the wild horse one more advantage. In June of 1993, Psycho, one of my favorite Assateague stallions, was seen eating fresh horse dung even though other foods were plentiful. I can only guess at the reasons for his behavior.

In order to be successful, a species must be able to compete with other wild animals. Throughout the western United States, the most common wild ungulate sharing range with wild horses is the mule deer. Their diets overlap something on the order of only 10%, so they compete little for food. The diets of wild horses and elk overlap much more, but since they usually find themselves living in very different habitats, competition is minimized. The browsing white-tailed deer of the coastal barrier islands offers almost no competition at all to the horse. This lack of competition with other wild ungulates is fortunate. If wild horses did compete with these species, all of which are valued game animals, there

would only be additional human pressures to reduce wild horse populations. There is trouble enough for free-roaming horses on our public lands, where they do compete with cattle for forage.

Water is, of course, critical to the survival of any species. Once again wild horses demonstrate an excellent ability to find water in those desolate corners that they are forced to call home. Horses frequently find water at springs, but these commonly dry up in some of the more arid sections of the West. During hot Pryor Mountain summers, the wild horses will sniff out damp areas in coulees and paw impressive holes into which water seeps. It can take more than an hour for a band to water, as the animals suck the seep's meager water. Pryor Mountain horses even venture into abandoned mines, walking far into the dark tunnels to locate standing groundwater that, although obviously contaminated with chemicals that have leached from the ground, appears to have no effect upon their health. In winter, wild horses can move onto otherwise arid grasslands by using snow as a water source.

On the barrier islands, fresh water is often completely absent, forcing the horses to drink saltwater of various concentrations. The horses of Assateague will not drink ocean water, but they have been observed drinking directly from the bay, which is only a fraction of the salinity of the ocean. Even the so-called freshwater ponds of the barrier islands are in reality somewhat saline. Barrier island horses use a resourceful strategy similar to that of their western counterparts to excavate damp areas,

On western wild horse ranges water is the single most important element of their habitat. Here, a group of lactating mares have watered first and moved on, while others take their turn.

pawing sizable holes next to ponds into which water seeps. I have never tested the salinity of these puddles, but the horses frequently go to all this effort rather than simply drink from the pond. It is also very interesting that I have never seen these horses drink from pools of fresh rainwater, which would be fairly free of salt.

Drinking saltwater causes the wild horses of Assateague to appear so bloated that it is sometimes difficult to tell a pregnant mare from a stallion solely on the basis of their girth. Because of the water's high salt concentration and the crystallized salt on the marsh grasses, these barrier island horses must drink every several hours, and they urinate about every three hours as well. On the other hand, the horses inhabiting the arid western ranges will often drink once a day or less and urinate only a few times a day.

Adaptability shows itself in wild horses in a variety of other ways, too. Insects can become a major physiological drain upon animals, and horses are particularly susceptible. It has been estimated that biting insects can rob a large ungulate of up to 500 cc of blood in a single day. No wild horses are free of biting insects, but those on barrier islands face especially dense hordes. Water becomes a refuge for these horses, and they will wade far out into the bay. At depths well above their stomachs they stand for hours enjoying relief from mosquitoes and biting flies. Sometimes they will actually wade so far out into the ocean surf that only their heads rise above the water. They use these water refuges largely between 10:00 A.M. and 4:00 P.M. As cool night falls and slows the insect, the horses wander back to the dunes to forage.

The biological costs of spending this much time just standing around in the water are significant. It reduces the time spent foraging and watering, and foals cannot nurse during the time spent at sea. Nevertheless, the benefits must balance these costs or these refuge-seeking behaviors would not be so common. Other strategies to avoid insects include hoof stomping, tail swishing in tight groups, and crashing through dense brush. One of the more interesting strategies I have witnessed also occurred on Assateague Island. All but a couple of miles of the island is a National Seashore, administered by the National Park Service. As such, the island is a wildlife sanctuary and the use of insecticides is prohibited because the activity is viewed as harmful to the environment. In the middle of the island is a two-mile stretch of campgrounds that is administered not by the National Park Service, but by the State of Maryland. This area is

sprayed weekly and has significantly fewer insects. On those summers when insects are particularly bad, bands of horses migrate to the park from as far away as six or seven miles. These bands tolerate one another to a far greater degree than at any other time of the year, although not all bands will make the annual migration. How many bands do decide to make use of the insect-free park depends on just how bad that year's insect crop is. Western range horses use grassy meadows early in the day, and as temperatures rise and insect numbers increase, they avoid them by moving to high, windswept ridges or use snowfields when available.

There also appears to be an elegant physiological adaptation to protect the young of the species from biting insects. On barrier islands, it has been noted that the greatest number of biting flies will land on harem stallions, an intermediate number upon mares, and the fewest number upon foals, the age group least able to tolerate the insect load. The most plausible explanation for this selective attraction of insects to stallions is probably some combination of both increased body temperature and sebaceous gland activity. Older horses have higher metabolic rates than younger horses, stallions higher than mares, and testosterone (the male sex hormone) stimulates sebaceous gland activity. Also, mature horses have more protein in their blood than do young horses, a fact that might make adult horse blood more attractive to flies. It seems that evolution has provided the vulnerable young horse with protection by reducing those factors that attract insects. A yet-to-be-tested theory suggests that foals may secrete some substance offensive to insects.

Another most remarkable adaptation was witnessed among Assateague's wild horses. Long before I had the opportunity to study these coastal barrier island horses, I spent many years observing the wild horses of Montana's Pryor Mountains, where the short forage is close to the ground and contains a good deal of grit. This grit produces fast wear to the horses' teeth. Along with other investigators, I have noticed that the jaws of dead animals almost always possessed teeth that were worn beyond their years. One would expect Assateague Island's sandy soil to produce equally heavy wear to horses' teeth. But I was to discover that this was not the case.

From my sand dune perch in the glow of a March sunset, I was watching a band of my favorite horses graze on dune grass when I noticed, for the first time, that every horse was shaking its head. Intrigued, I watched more closely and saw that the horses were knocking sand from

Horses have eyes with a special anatomical arrangement of the lens that permits them to focus on the grass they are eating as well as objects in the distance—both at the same time.

the roots of the dune grass clumps by whisking them back and forth across the branches of bayberry bushes. They were cleaning the sand from their food! I have since noticed that while almost all the wild horses of Assateague do this, few wild horses on western lands have picked up this clever adaptive behavior, indicating it is not innate. There must be a wonderful but forever secret story of how the first wild horse of this island learned to clean sand from its food and an equally fascinating story of how the others learned this behavior, incorporating it into their routine.

Even the vision of the wild horse is adapted for survival. Without a doubt vision is the horses' greatest sensory asset. They can see objects at astounding distances and apparently with remarkable clarity. In open range country an alert stallion may spot other horses up to two miles away. But the horse is a grazer, and it spends a lot of time with its head in the grass, a potentially dangerous habit if predators are present. To compensate, the eyes of the horse have evolved at the sides of the head, providing a very wide field of vision. Additionally, the retina and the lens of each eye are specially arranged so that both the grass upon which the horse is grazing and distant objects are in focus at the very same time. Thus, the horse can graze, pay attention to grasses only inches away, and at the same time keep a wary and focused eye on its more distant surroundings. Over the years I have found that it is very difficult to sneak up on a horse. Not only do horses have superb visual acuity, they also possess excellent night vision, permitting nocturnal activity that differs little from that of day.

These are but a few of the adaptations that have made the wild horse such an exceptionally successful species. If my theory that the horse is one of the world's most successful wildlife species has any merit, then we should be able to test that idea and predict that wild horses can be found worldwide, in just about every type of habitat imaginable. It is not possible to identify every wild horse population in the world here—there are simply too many—but we can get an overall picture of the immense range of habitat. Let us first start with the wild horses of North America.

In the United States, wild horses inhabit public lands in nine western states and East Coast barrier islands, with smaller numbers inhabiting some state parks in the central portion of the country. The majority of wild horses in the United States, somewhere around 50,000,

Winter snows provide a plentiful source of water and permit horses to expand their home ranges into regions where water was not available during the summer months. As free-standing water disappears, the horses will eat snow.

are found in Nevada, southeastern Oregon, central Idaho, Utah, southern Montana, western North Dakota, western Colorado, northern California, and Wyoming. The majority, probably 35,000, live in Nevada. The habitats in which they live are diverse, but most can be characterized as semiarid desert. A few of the wild horse ranges, including those near Challis, Idaho, the Pryor Mountains in Montana, and Montgomery Pass, on the California-Nevada Border, include reasonably high mountains, ranging up to 9,000 feet.

Two of these populations, the Pryor Mountain horses of Montana, and the Kiger Plateau horses of Oregon, have often been touted as original Spanish mustangs. They are very small, have a dorsal stripe running the length of their back, and have a great deal of "tiger striping" on their legs, a pattern indicating a primitive type of horse. On these two ranges, the predominant colors are dun (neutral brown to a dull gray brown), buckskin, grulla (gray—often with black faces), some red and blue roans, blacks, bays (dark brown with black mane and tail) and sorrels (lighter brown with light or blond mane and tail). The ears are often outlined in black. The Pryor horses often show up with only five lumbar vertebrae, or with the fifth and sixth fused, another sign of old breeds (Arabians have only five). However, many of the Pryor horses show some physical traits of the draft horse, and the broad white faces of the Kiger horses are inconsistent with pure Spanish blood. In the case of the Kiger horses, it is highly unlikely that any pure line of Spanish horse could have survived without interbreeding with the 300,000 to 400,000 wild horses thought to have been in residence in southeastern Oregon during the early years of this century. The unlikely probability that they are "pure" descendants of the first wave of Spanish horses need not detract from their beauty, their tenacity as a species, or our appreciation of them.

Equally intriguing arguments are heard in some quarters speculating that perhaps the North American horse did not become extinct. If some remnant populations of the horse living in North America 12,000 years ago survived, the North American wild horse would in fact be a native species. Supporters theorize that the few small groups that may have survived in remote areas of the west eventually mingled with those horses introduced

WILD HORSES IN THE U.S.A.

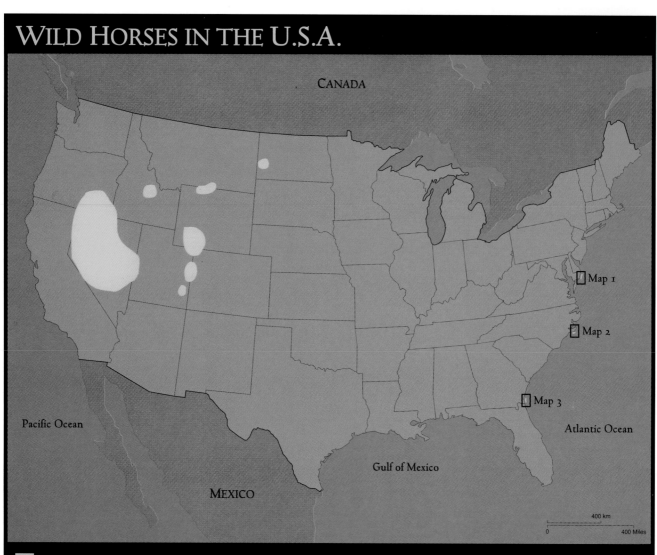

CANADA

Pacific Ocean

MEXICO

Gulf of Mexico

Atlantic Ocean

Map 1

Map 2

Map 3

400 km

0   400 Miles

■ = LOCATIONS OF LARGEST HERDS OF WILD HORSES IN THE U.S.A. UNDER BLM OR NPS MANAGEMENT

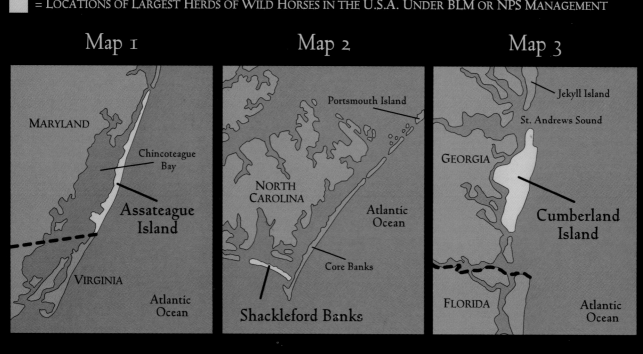

Map 1

MARYLAND

Chincoteague
Bay

Assateague
Island

VIRGINIA

Atlantic
Ocean

Map 2

Portsmouth Island

NORTH
CAROLINA

Atlantic
Ocean

Core Banks

Shackleford Banks

Map 3

Jekyll Island

St. Andrews Sound

GEORGIA

Cumberland
Island

FLORIDA

Atlantic
Ocean

here 400 years ago. Part of me wishes this was true and that it could be proved. It would help end the discrimination of horses as exotics by ranchers, and by federal and state agencies that claim wild horses compete with domestic livestock and game animals. Unfortunately, there is no hard proof for or against the idea.

The theory of a "native" North American horse notwithstanding, the East Coast barrier island horses are some of the continent's oldest and include herds living on Assateague Island, off the coasts of Maryland and Virginia; Ocracoke Island and the Shackleford Banks of North Carolina; and Cumberland Island and several other islands off the coast of Georgia. The range of climatic conditions, quality of nutrition, and other factors influencing living conditions is extreme, but the wild horses have nevertheless thrived.

In Canada, wild horses range from the southern Yukon Territory, through British Columbia, down through the Rocky Mountain foothills of western Alberta, and on Sable Island, off the coast of Nova Scotia. Once we get south of the U.S. border, we find them in Mexico and throughout South America, including Brazil, Argentina, and many other countries. Looking west from the New World, we find sizable populations in the Kaimanawa Mountains of New Zealand and outright staggering numbers in the Northern Territories of Australia. The New Zealand populations were derived from Exmoor ponies, Welsh stallions, and cavalry horses. The Australian populations are estimated to be as high as 600,000, but they fluctuate with the rains and droughts. These wild horses, known locally as brumbies, or Walers (derived from the release of military stock from New South Wales), live in one of the harshest environments on the face of the Earth, but their numbers alone tell of their success.

The Misaki wild horses of southern Japan date back to the 1600s, and western China and Mongolia have unknown numbers of wild horses on the windswept steppes. Scattered remnant populations of wild horses can be found in South Africa. On continental Europe, the best known wild horses reside on the estuary of the Rhone River of France, in a swampy area known as the Camargue. Across the channel, in Great Britain, we find wild horses all across the country, with exotic names such as the Exmoor pony, the Dartmoor pony, and the New Forest pony. The Exmoor pony is thought to be the oldest of the breeds, and there are some who believe that the Exmoor represents a native species. The most widely accepted theory is that the native British wild pony of 100,000 years ago was hunted to extinction during the Mesolithic and Neolithic periods, but some believe it survived intact and escaped extinction. This theory, as with the similar one put forth about North American horses, cannot be proved or disproved.

One needs only to examine a map of the world—some sort of an atlas that lists climates, rainfall, temperatures, and altitudes—to understand that the wild horse knows few barriers. Because we have relegated the horse largely to poor-quality lands, it has been tested under the most trying conditions. Only the most adaptable species could have achieved this remarkable worldwide success.

Of all the large mammals, only the horse has achieved this feat.

FAMILY LIFE AMONG WILD HORSES

On a high ridge in the Pryor Mountains lived a band of horses typical in many ways. They eked out a living in this foreboding place, six miles of desolate, knife-edged rock so very sharp at its crest that a man has all he can do to keep from falling off. Few trees grow on hot and barren Syke's Ridge, and despite the land's bleak nature, this band of horses clattered among the mountain mahogany.

Led by a large sorrel stallion with a broad, white blaze on his face, this little band of seven or eight horses had one distinction. They had adopted into their society a most unusual member: a bighorn sheep ram.

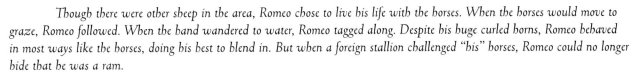

Though there were other sheep in the area, Romeo chose to live his life with the horses. When the horses would move to graze, Romeo followed. When the band wandered to water, Romeo tagged along. Despite his huge curled horns, Romeo behaved in most ways like the horses, doing his best to blend in. But when a foreign stallion challenged "his" horses, Romeo could no longer hide that he was a ram.

As the sorrel herd stallion postured and fought with an intruder stallion, Romeo would dance excitedly about the combatants on his short sheep legs. Shadowboxing the intruder, Romeo would rear up and crash forward with his impressive curled horns in the manner in which his species fights. Though he never made contact with the stallion, he clearly imagined he was valiantly participating in the battle. When the raider was vanquished, Romeo would proudly prance alongside the herd stallion as they both returned to the band, and the herd would welcome their conquering heroes.

I had long understood that horses were extremely social. But until I studied the Syke's Ridge band I would have never dreamed that they would choose to so casually accept another species, especially one as strange as Romeo—the ram that thought he was a horse.

elatively few humans give much thought to the social organization of most wildlife species, perhaps because of our intensely egocentric view of the world. We tend to think of animals' relationships—and their behavioral reactions—to humans, but we consider animals' relationships to each other less often. We know that wolves run in packs, or that certain birds live in flocks, or that some large animals run in herds, but beyond that we tend to overlook the complexity of the social order within those various groups.

In the case of wild horses, our understanding is tainted by our perceptions of domestic horses. Seldom does anyone get to see a "natural" group of horses on the farm or ranch. The stallions are usually castrated (gelded) and as such do not behave like typical male horses. If someone harbors genuine intact stallions, they are usually kept apart from the mares except for breeding. Young horses are removed from their mothers at an early age, and we almost never get to see a herd of horses from one ranch confront a herd of horses from another ranch. When unfamiliar horses do get to meet, they usually have a human sitting upon them, prompting them to act in ways that are entirely alien to their species.

Put another way, the behavior of the domestic horse is an artifact, under which is buried millions of years of behavioral evolution. Other than Przewalski's horses, true wild horses disappeared before man began recording history, obscuring the true picture of horse social behavior. Only the modern wild horse can give us a glimpse of its social evolution.

A good starting point for understanding the social organization of wild horses is a consideration of territoriality. Among the living species of *Equidae*, Grevy's zebra, the wild ass (*E. africanus*), the Asiatic wild ass (*E. hemionus*), and the feral donkey (*E. asinus*) are territorial. They will define a discrete territory and they will defend it against others of their species. Both sexes of territorial equids will travel about alone or in groups, but these groups are unstable and will constantly change in size and composition. The stallions establish and defend a physical territory.

The wild horse, on the other hand, is non-territorial. This species will not define and defend a territory. Rather, the wild horse will have a home range which may or may not overlap with the home ranges of other wild horses. Instead, the wild horse has what some refer to as a "sphere of intolerance," an area of space within which other horse groups may not enter without eliciting an aggressive response. This "sphere of intolerance" differs from territory in that it moves with the horse band.

This particular arrangement, peculiar to the non-territorial wild equids, is thought to be a more advanced type of social organization than that found among the territorial equids. It is adaptive in that it allows the wild horse to range over greater areas of land and therefore to seek more diverse sources of food or to move to areas where climatic conditions are better. The home ranges of wild horses vary according to the habitat in which we find the animals. In areas of the western United States, where there is a great deal of space and forage is sparse, home ranges of harem bands may be as large as 80 square miles.

Until three years of age, young stallions have a good relationship with their harem band stallion, which is also usually their father. Then, the harem stallion runs the young stallions out of the band. (overleaf) Wild horses are not territorial, but when they encroach upon one another's bands, the stallions will engage in a great deal of lively posturing and sometimes even outright combat. These two stallions are engaged in the posturing that usually precedes a fight.

Horses on a barrier island may have a home range as small as three square miles. Although wild horses no longer inhabit the Grand Canyon, their home ranges there were calculated to be over 800 square miles. It is interesting that no correlation has ever been found between band size and size of home range.

The one exception to this rule of non-territorialism has been noted on two barrier islands off the East Coast of the United States. Several bands of horses living on a very narrow and sparsely vegetated section of Shackleford Banks have displayed true territorial behavior by defining and defending a territorial boundary. A single stallion named Comma, from Assateague Island's north end, has recently displayed the same territorial behaviors. Defending a defined line from the ocean to the bay, Comma springs into action and attempts to run off intruding horses. The exceptions of Comma and those bands on Shackleford Banks are thought to be caused by a combination of the narrowness of the islands and the ability of the horses to view all other horse activity. In other words, the narrowness of the island is less than the "sphere of intolerance." Other Assateague horses that live on sections where the ocean-bay distance is greater, and where dense vegetation makes seeing difficult, demonstrate non-territorial behavior.

The social organization of the wild horse is as complex as the horse is beautiful. When we think of a herd of horses, most of us imagine those gatherings of thousands, such as those that live in western states like Nevada. These large groups are not cohesive units, for within these herds there are separate bands. This basic social group is also known as a harem band and may be as small as two horses, though it sometimes exceeds twenty. The average is closer to five to seven. Each band contains a sexually mature stallion that is usually between seven and twenty years old. The band will also contain anywhere from one to fifteen adult mares between the ages of two and twenty or more years. One- and two-year-old juveniles and foals of the year make up the remainder of the band. As opposed to the loose organization among territorial wild equids, the harem band is so very stable and cohesive the mares often stay together even after their stallion dies.

It is important to understand, however, that a "typical" band exists only in our minds. For example, while most wild horse bands across North America and around the world will have only a single sexually mature stallion, in some rare instances there will be up to three. Most of the 14 North American herds studied during the 1970s and 1980s had a single stallion, yet many of the horse bands of Wyoming's Red Desert had two stallions. We do not fully understand why these differences occur. It may have to do with sex ratios in the population or perhaps the way in which a band first forms. However, even in the exceptional bands with more than one stallion, one is always dominant. He will prevent subordinate stallions from displaying certain stallion behaviors, such as herding.

On Assateague Island I witnessed several young bachelor stallions raiding a harem band and running off a few mares. In several instances, two or more young males kept the company of one of the stolen mares. In one example, four stallions peacefully coexisted with a single young mare for over a year ("Double-O" later died giving birth to a foal), and on another occasion, two young stallions lived with a single bay mare. In the latter case, the pinto stallion we knew as Little Sebastian remained close by her side almost all of the time, while the second stallion, a sorrel, remained 50 to 100 yards away. When this little unorthodox band was threatened by another stallion, the sorrel did all the posturing and fighting, while clever Little Sebastian ran off with the mare. After the fight, they would reassemble in their strange little band. It is important, in the light of such exceptions, that we not allow a single view of a wild horse band at some point in time to give us false impressions. The true nature of the wild horse is something that is learned only from continual observation over an extended period of time.

The harem stallion's superiority has been demonstrated by his ability to compete with and defeat other males. He must be tough, aggressive, and intelligent in order to gain a harem, and the costs of winning are usually written in the scars all over his muscular body. He acquired his harem of mares in one of a number of ways. If he was lucky, he might have been wandering along, minding his business, and just stumbled across some mares whose own herd stallion had finally died. More likely, he raided another harem band, and in the confusion of mares running about, managed to run far enough away with a mare that the harem stallion dared not follow, lest he lose more mares to still other young bachelor stallions.

Before the young stallion acquires his own harem however, he passes through several years of what I like to refer to as horse adolescence. During this time he is almost always a part of another basic unit of horse social order, the bachelor band. After three relatively carefree years in the company of his mother and other band companions, his life changes abruptly.

The young stallion may, if he is lucky or wise, leave the band on his own accord, without any interference by the band stallion. Many two- or three-year-olds choose to strike out on their own in this manner.

Others who choose not to leave voluntarily face a traumatic exit. Usually with the onset of the breeding season, and at approximately the young stallion's third birthday, the harem stallion becomes aggressive and drives him from the band, sometimes brutally, with a barrage of kicks and bites. The process might take several weeks, and the young bewildered stallion receives no help from former companions or even his mother. Up until this difficult time in his life the young stallion had a good relationship with the harem stallion. They would often spend time grooming one another or even neck wrestling, and the suddenness of the change in behavior must come as something of a shock. However, as with all maturing male animals, his own behavior changes, too. As he approaches his third spring, he grows aggressive and desires to attend fertile mares who have suddenly become very interesting.

The young stallion's changes are triggered by dramatic increases in the male sex hormone, testosterone. In most stallions, testosterone increases occur during their third spring. However, on two occasions we have witnessed two-year-olds with dramatic hormone increases being ejected from the band. The young stallion's carefree days of youth are gone, and as he asserts his sexual maturity, the herd stallion grows intolerant of this young male's presence. Finally genuine hostility erupts, and the young stallion's remaining days as a member of the band of his birth are numbered.

Following his ejection, the young stallion follows the band for several weeks, seeking its hospitality and comfort. Each time he gets too close, he is run off again. Finally, usually by pure coincidence, he will run into a group of young males, ranging in age from three to perhaps eight. For the first time in weeks he is not chased away. He is instead greeted with curiosity and perhaps even charity. Mutual grooming will occur, they will travel together over long distances, feed together, and in general develop a loose social order of their own. This bachelor band is not as stable as the harem band. It will often break into smaller groups, only to later rejoin. There are no cooperative efforts to raid harems, and the companionship of the bachelor band reflects the social nature of the horse. At some point, however, the bachelor stallion will find opportunity knocking at his door and he will, by one means or another, acquire his own mares.

The bachelor stallion's chances of acquiring a harem band of his own are in large part dependent upon his social rank within his bachelor band. Social ranks among mares are sometimes transient and hard to determine, but there is a definite and clear social order within bachelor bands. Not surprisingly, it is the highest-ranking bachelor stallion that usually acquires mares first. Thus, the years in the bachelor band are formative years, in which developing social behaviors determine the degree of success later in life. The bachelor stallion's position in the bachelor band may be predetermined to some degree. Some who have studied wild horses believe that dominant mares significantly affect their offspring's behavior and that dominant mares tend to produce dominant stallions.

This remains an untested idea, but I have witnessed this phenomenon in a band of horses on Assateague Island. A young stallion, designated by us as N9H, gathered a harem band at four years of age, an unusually young age to become a harem stallion.

His mother was an extremely dominant mare and one has to wonder if all this was coincidental. Some stallions, however, will never acquire a harem band of their own and will pass through their lives in the company of other bachelor stallions.

When a young stallion obtains his first mare he is the picture of attentiveness. All of a sudden nothing in his life seems as important to this young stallion as his new companion. He will nicker constantly, crowd at her side, nuzzle her, and follow her everywhere. Unless the relationship is threatened by another stallion, he will generally let her wander wherever she wants, remaining right behind her. The young stallion's grazing time will decrease as his attentions now focus only upon the mare. Slowly, over some period of time, he will become a bit less attentive, though no less protective, but each new mare he acquires will receive the same initial attention.

In October 1990 I discovered a fine young bay stallion on the marshes of Assateague. A bump the size of a marble on the end of his nose earned him the name Wart. Wart had just acquired a handsome-looking two-year-old pinto mare we named Cutthroat, for the white slash across her neck. It was obvious that Cutthroat was Wart's first mare, and they spent hours nuzzling, nickering and making amazing facial expressions. But what intrigued me the most were their periodic and spontaneous two-mile runs. Side by side they would race south to Tingle's Island and back along an old back country road. Each day they took this giddy romp for no apparent reason other than the sheer joy of racing the wind in each other's company.

Once a young stallion acquires his own band, he faces new problems. Not all mares are happy in their new social groups. They probably miss their companions from the old band or perhaps one of their younger offspring. Two mares who have spent most of their lives together may get cranky and uncooperative when separated. The newly acquired mare can spend a great deal of time trying to escape her new harem stallion to rejoin her old friend. The young stallion with his first harm will face threats from his recent companions, the young bachelor stallions, or from the herd stallion from which he pilfered his mares.

Wild stallions' tremendous eyesight often detects the presence of other horses from over a mile away. A challenge will bring the two stallions racing at high speed toward each other, meeting with tails held aloft. Tensely the two approach to sniff at each other's nostrils. This is usually followed by both animals defecating. Each will then sniff at the other's dung pile while standing nonchalantly side by side. This is only a prelude to the fireworks. In an instant the stallions begin screaming, biting, and kicking, going at each other ferociously for a half minute or more. Most bites are directed at the legs of the opponent, presumably to sever tendons. Then they will stop, defecate again, and begin the cycle all over again. Depending upon the tenacity of the horses, this may go on for many minutes, until one loses his enthusiasm for the conflict. Turning tail, the unsuccessful stallion will trot off to tend to his bruised body and injured psyche. The wounds suffered are usually not serious and fatalities are extremely rare. During these fierce fights, the mares and the immature horses continue their activities with little obvious interest in the harem stallion's tribulations.

A stallion requires wit as well as brawn to protect his harem from other stallions. During the late fall and winter months, the band will tend to spread out more than usual—the harem stallion allows the mares to wander farther from the band. Over most of North America, the breeding season of March through June requires the stallion to keep his band tightly together. He positions his band in such a way that they can be protected from the advances of other stallions when the "horse wars" of spring begin.

One particular Assateague Island harem stallion developed two rather ingenious devices to defend his harem. Scotty, as I know him, has a habit, when threatened by other stallions, of herding his mares between the steel guard rails of the causeway to the island. With his mares safely confined behind him, he simply patrols the 50 feet between the rails. His other defensive plan is to herd his mares, usually around midday,

The white herd stallion, with ears back and malice intended, runs off a group of bachelor stallions who have come too close to his mare and her new foal.

into a wooden corral in a state park on the island. This corral was originally built to provide a picnic area off-limits to the panhandling of horses and has since been washed away by storms. The corral had only a single entrance and was planted in grass. Once the mares were safely inside the corral and contentedly grazing, the stallion would lie down across the narrow entrance and drift off to sleep. A strange stallion would have to step on him before he could gain access to the mares. No stallion was successful in breaching Scotty's defenses during my four years of observation.

As with most aspects of life, all things change, and the successful harem stallion is at best delaying the inevitable. One day he will be challenged and he will lose. There is an old axiom that there is always someone on the block who is tougher than you, and so it is with wild horses. Deposed harem stallions usually face a

short and lonely life, particularly if they are older, for they seldom join young lone males or bachelor groups. Perhaps because they are already old and near the end of their lives, most do not live for more than a few years after being defeated. But I strongly suspect that the stress of living alone for the first time in their lives hastens the end.

Put yourself in the hooves of a young Pryor Mountain stallion. Born into a band, you've lived your life among many other horses. At age three, although the harem stallion rudely runs you off from the band and separates you from the only companions you have ever known, you find comfort with other equine soul mates who have suffered the same fate. You join your new acquaintances in a bachelor band. While it is not as cohesive as the harem band, you enjoy the companionship of other horses. And later, when you are perhaps seven or *(above) Once a young bachelor stallion acquires his first mare he is extremely attentive to her. This young Wyoming stallion will stay close to his new companion. (right) Bachelor bands are made up of younger stallions that have been kicked out of their natal bands and group together for companionship. They find comfort in this association and develop clear dominance hierarchies. It is a time of learning and preparing for the future.*

eight and in the prime of life, you masterfully acquire a harem band of your own. Though guarding them is sometimes tedious, you are rewarded with the companionship of your mares and sons and daughters. And then one dark day, when you are fourteen or fifteen, you are challenged and defeated. Driven off by the victor, you find yourself not only alone but alone forever.

Horses are remarkably gregarious and social, and the horse alone is not a happy animal. Stress begets disease, opening the door to death. By our standards it sounds cruel, but it is nature's way of ensuring that only the fittest can pass on their genes. Such is the life of the wild stallion.

The mare is truly the heart of the wild horse social order, and it is clear we still do not understand all the subtleties of their remarkable array of relationships. The stallion, because he is usually the only sexually mature stallion in the band, must define his roles and status only in terms of his adult mares and the juveniles. Mares, however, must contend with the stallion, the juveniles, and one another. As such, the mare's relationships are more complex, for she must develop a social hierarchy relative to other mares as well as to the harem stallion.

There are two considerations when examining the social relationships between horses of a band: social dominance and leadership. They are not always synonymous. Social dominance, which implies a high position in the pecking order and priority access to resources, should not be confused with simple aggression. For example, if two mares come upon a choice clump of grass at the same time, the dominant animal will get the prize. When the dominant mare makes her move to eat the grass, the subordinate mare will usually back away or move to another clump. Studies with domestic mares have demonstrated that there is no correlation between dominance and ability to learn—or horse intelligence, as some would view this subject. Leadership, on the other hand, implies a horse who will determine many of the day-to-day activities and time budgets for the band.

If this were all not complicated enough, horses from different geographic regions demonstrate different strategies regarding social rank and leadership. While a mare might be the leader during one set of circumstances, the stallion will become the leader during another set of circumstances. Among Pryor Mountain wild horses, the stallion is almost always the dominant animal in the band and the leader in better than half of the bands. He herds animals off to watering holes and moves them back to feeding areas. In contrast, in Assateague Island bands the stallion is rarely the dominant animal and is the leader only during encroachments by other stallions, giving both of these other responsibilities to one of the mares in the band.

The causes of these regional differences are not fully understood; however, the length of time the stallion has been residing in the band may play an important role. The Pryor Mountain harem stallions generally enjoy long tenure, and their dominance over almost all mares on the social ladder may reflect their long-standing presence. Many harem stallions studied on Assateague were short-timers and were in control of the bands only a short time prior to our dominance hierarchy studies. Thus, the length of time a stallion has been in charge of a band may be the deciding factor as to whether the stallion or some of the mares will be the dominant animals.

What makes a mare a dominant animal? To be truthful, no one really knows, but age and size seem to have the greatest bearing. A larger mare tends to move up in rank, and if she is older than other animals, she tends to move up also. Neither pregnancy nor the presence of a foal increases a mare's chances of rising in the social order. Subordinate mares lower on the social ladder are subject to aggressive acts from the other mares. And subordinate mares with foals seem to sink even lower on the social order yardstick. Beyond these generalizations, other factors can play important roles in determining who is the boss. The length of time a mare, or a stallion, has resided in a particular band appears to impart some advantage, and a smaller or younger mare who has been in a band for a long period of time may be dominant over a larger or older mare who has only recently joined the band. As the size of the harem band increases, the intensity of the struggle to define social order increases. The larger the band, the more frequent is aggressiveness.

The same is true for stallions. Their position on the band's social register is strongly tied to the length of their tenure as harem stallion. Dominant mares don't receive special attention from the stallion. He tends to participate equally in mutual grooming with all his mares. All these considerations of dominance, leadership, and who serves as boss may create a picture of daily mayhem in the band. Nothing could be further from the truth. The wild horse band is a picture of tranquility when one views it over the long term. The need to be together transcends the complicated social hierarchies of wild horse family life.

Despite some differences between horses in different parts of the world, most wild horse herds are composed of harem bands that are directed by "lead mares"—older, or larger, but definitely dominant animals. These mares appear to make the day-to-day decisions about where and when to feed and water. As the band approaches a water hole in single file, there will be a rough approximation of leadership and/or dominance, with the lead mare out in front. When watering, lactating mares will sometimes take the lead, probably because of their great need to replace lost fluids. Unless threatened, the harem stallion will take up a position near the rear of the band and seemingly play little role in decision-making.

Leadership roles change as conditions change. With the onset of the reproductive season, stallions play a larger leadership role, usually in two distinct contexts. First, the stallion will often take over decision-making about the day-to-day movements of the band, being careful to place his group of mares as far away from other bands and in the most defensible positions as possible. The stallion will also become more sensitive to how spread out the band is while grazing. When mares exceed some predetermined distance from the stallion, he institutes "snaking" or herding behavior. Ears go back, his neck arches and his head drops toward the ground, and he will begin to circle the offending mare and get between her and the wide open spaces beyond. The mare responds with a quick return to the band, and sometimes the mere sight of the stallion's posture is enough to correct her errant ways and bring her home at a run. The more exaggerated the stallion's herding posture, the more dramatic the results.

Mares, too, leave the band of their birth at some point. The departure of the mares is primarily voluntary, and it is interesting that immature mares, or those in the early years of sexual maturity, leave the band with the greatest frequency.

This Pryor Mountain harem stallion attends to his mares with equal frequency.

Some investigators have suggested that the young mares do not always leave the band voluntarily but are forced out. In either case, their departure prevents inbreeding between a stallion and his daughter or between brother and sister. Other mares may leave from time to time, and up to 30 percent of the adult mares may change bands in a given year on some ranges. Most changes among mares occur during the winter, when the stallion is least vigilant. These mares often wander off and after a few days or weeks simply walk up to and join a new band. Though the stallion will show some interest, and the band's mares will nervously approach her, tensions will ease quickly as the new mare finds her place in the band. Exchanges of mares during the breeding season are impossible, as the ever-watchful stallion prevents any mares, mature or immature, from leaving.

Why adult mares move between bands is not understood, but my own observations suggest that it has a lot to do with the mare's personality. One of my favorite wild horses on Assateague Island is a nine-year-old mare whom we call Scotty's Girl. Over the eight years I observed this horse, she wandered from band to band more often than I can remember. It appears that when she has become tired or bored with a band she simply takes off up the island and finds some new companions. This mare moves with more frequency than most and I shall probably never know why. If there is such a thing among horses, Scotty's Girl is truly liberated.

Yet some mares live their entire adult lives in one band. The stallions change, but the mares do not. Not only do the mares retain the band's identity when a stallion dies, but more often than not they determine the home range of the band. Two of my favorite mares on Assateague Island are T2BE (13 years old) and M17G (11 years old). I don't know exactly how long they have been living together but they have been inseparable for the nine years I have known them. They were both part of a band we knew as the Bayside Bunch, and they had a very well-defined home range in the vicinity of Bayside (below) *A young Oregon stallion displays "snaking" or herding behavior, with neck arched down and ears back, in order to move his mares back toward the band. Even the sight of this posture will cause mares to quickly return to their band. (right) A stallion nuzzles one of his mares. The social relationship between the horses of a band is close, affectionate, and far more complex than one might imagine.*

Campground. In 1989 their stallion, Zorro, died from equine encephalitis. For the first year after his death, several stallions attempted to take control of these rather dominant mares, but in each case they simply ran off and returned to their original home range near the campground. A rather headstrong stallion that we knew as Hot Air Balloon—named for a balloon's likeness on his side—managed to become their harem stallion. He took control of the two mares during the summer months, and the three horses lived in and around Bayside Camp-ground. Normally Hot Air Balloon spent his winters in the marshes about four miles south of Bayside, and we were all interested to see if he would be able to move his mares southward down the island to his original home range. Who would you bet on? Hot Air Balloon was no match for these two mares, and he spent the winter in their home range. Thus, it appears that mares have a strong attachment to the home range of their birth.

Some mares also reflect a conscious attempt at selecting their own stallions. On several occasions I or my students have witnessed certain mares trying to join the band of a particular stallion. Other studies show that mares with foals move more frequently between bands than mares without, and subordinate mares transfer with more frequency than dominant mares. It also appears that the longer the stallion has been with the band, the fewer the exchanges of mares.

It is clear that wild horses do most things together. Horses of a particular band graze or rest at the same times of the day, as well as take water and travel together. Their activities are highly coordinated. Only foals act independently. They are not yet aware of the patterns and need more rest than other horses. But as they become older, they catch on to the patterns and adjust to the band's daily routines. The foal's relationship to the band stallion varies and, I believe, reflects the personality of the stallion more than anything else. Some stallions show little interest, while others will spend considerable time investigating foals. Some stallions even engage in play behavior.

Social order among individual animals within a band is only one aspect of the dominance hierarchy of wild horses. Another is interband dominance relationships. For many years we have tended to think of wild horse herds—as opposed to harem or bachelor bands—as mere aggregations of horses, with little thought to how bands might interact. However, it appears that there is a social order among the bands themselves. Nowhere are band hierarchies more apparent than around water sources. On the Red Desert of Wyoming, there was a clear rank among bands waiting to gain access to water holes, with the highest-ranking bands watering first, and the lowest ranking bands waiting long periods of time before watering. The bands apparently could recognize the social rank of one another, and both stallions and mares participated in aggressive actions in asserting social rank.

Large bands tend to be more dominant. At a saltwater estuary near Beaufort, North Carolina, social

rank at water holes was determined by the herd's length of residency in that area. We have already seen that wild horses have home ranges that move from area to area, and in times of decreasing water sources, the home ranges of many wild horse bands can overlap substantially. The band that normally lived near the water source was found to be the most dominant band when competition increased. Thus, there is a concept of "ownership" among wild horse bands. In both these cases of interband social rank, we are forced to consider the entire herd as a structured social unit rather than just a group of horses broken up into small bands.

Wild horses are one of the most social animals in nature. The complexity of their social organization is extreme. Their social relationships and well-defined social order are based on the horses knowing one another *really* well. We still do not understand all the nuances or origins of this behavior, but we can appreciate these animals more fully if we simply recognize that they interact in complex ways. Equally important, today's wild horses give us important clues to the social evolution of their wild ancestors. Perhaps just as important, they also give us important messages, if we take the time to listen, about the social needs of their domestic cousins.

REPRODUCTION

For almost all of March I had been following the band of N6EI, one of the prettiest of all Assateague mares, through the thick loblolly pines of their range. N6EI's shyness made spotting her in the jungle of pines an especially difficult task. Still, as winter's dampness bowed to the warmth of spring, I was able to study the band and this lovely pinto mare despite the challenges of her tangled home.

As I prepared to leave the island near the end of March for a two-week trip to the mainland, I noticed the N6EI had seemingly disappeared. This was more than just her normal secrecy. The pinto was utterly absent. I wondered about it the whole time I was gone, hoping that perhaps I just hadn't noticed her as she kept furtively to the dense forest. When I returned in mid-April and learned that she had not yet reappeared, I grew worried.

Soon after, as I waded through the tall reeds and grasses of the marsh behind our little Park Service cabin, I was startled to see something white moving through the nearby greenbrier jungle. I paused and watched, and as I did, pretty little N6EI pranced out into the slough and whinnied softly. She looked over her back expectantly. As shyly as his mother, a gangly male foal emerged from the brush.

N6EIM (so named using his mother's four symbols and M to designate 1988, the year of his birth) gamboled uncertainly on new legs. I smiled to see what must have been some of his very first wobbling steps and noticed as the two of them turned from me that the bloody signs of birth were still splattered on his mother's rump. I knew then that N6EI must have left her band as her time grew near and that her shy nature prompted her to choose a safe and private birthing spot deep in the protective greenbrier.

I was relieved and pleased. As had been repeated so often in the past 300 years, a new horse had come to beautiful Assateague Island.

No single biological characteristic is more important to a species than the ability to successfully reproduce. When considering wildlife, we tend to think in terms of individual animals rather than populations, and successful reproduction is not necessarily a requirement for an individual animal to live out its life. After all, most people have their own pets neutered, and even domestic horse owners have stallions gelded, so it is natural for us to overlook the importance of reproduction. Survival of an individual is not very important to a species. Rather, the reproductive success of a population decides if the species is to survive.

In the western United States and on East Coast barrier islands, wild horse populations increase on average by 10 to 20% per year, differing from herd to herd and from year to year, dependent mostly upon the severity of winters. A herd's growth rate is controlled by the average life span of its animals (particularly the reproductive life span of the females), the age at which the females become reproductive, the birth rate, the survival rate of the young, and overall mortality. These factors in turn are controlled by the physiology of the animals, the weather, the nutrition, herd density, and any other conditions that might influence mortality rates, such as predation.

Compared to other wild long-lived large mammals, the 10 to 20% growth rate of wild horse herds is considered very high. Other species of wild ungulates, such as elk and bison, achieve growth rates this high only when the herds are growing. We can conclude from wild horse herd growth rates that most of these herds probably have not achieved their maximum size. We can also conclude that one factor of herd growth—reproduction—is successful by any measure.

The wild horse is a seasonal breeder. In the northern hemisphere the breeding season occurs between late March and July, and it seems this season does not change appreciably regardless of the latitude of the herd. In some other ungulates, such as the white-tailed deer, the farther north, the more compressed the season, and the farther south, the more expanded the season—but that is not the case with wild horses. Their reproductive season is triggered by day length, or photoperiod, as it is known to biologists. This contrasts with a number of common wild ungulates, like deer, elk and bison, that mate as day lengths decrease. In New Zealand and Australia, most horses breed in November and December, the time of increasing day lengths in the southern hemisphere.

The length of the breeding season appears to be determined by the amount of time the particular wild horse herd has been living in a true free-roaming condition. For example, among the Pryor Mountain horses, which have been free-roaming for more than 200 years, there is almost a complete absence of foals born before March or after August. In contrast, the horses of Nevada's Granite Range—free-roaming only since the Great Depression—produce some foals year-round. If we examine the months of the year when ovulation, breeding, and foaling occur among domestic horses in the northern hemisphere, we find that—while there is a clear seasonal pattern around April, May, and June—successful reproduction can and does occur almost all year long. Domestic mares on good nutrition will breed well into

Growth rates for North American wild horse herds have been unusually high compared to those of other large hoofed species like deer or elk. Growth of a wild horse population is regulated by nutrition, climate, mortality, and birth rates.

(below) As the breeding season approaches, the stallion becomes less tolerant of mares who wander too far from the band. This stallion displays herding behavior posture, and his mares heed his warning, returning in a hurry. (right) Foal mortality is quite high during some years, usually because of severe weather. It is very important to be born late enough in the season to miss spring snows and early enough to grow as large as possible before winter storms.

the fall and some will breed as late as November or December. That seems to be the case with some wild horses, too. Many years ago we noticed that domestic mares were producing foals from January through October, while wild mares from the Pryor Mountains and Winemucca, Nevada, were producing their foals almost exclusively between April and July. What could account for these differences? Was it nutrition alone?

The mare is considered to be seasonally polyestrus, a term that means the mare has recurring ovulations during a particular season. Previous studies had already demonstrated that populations of domestic mares will ovulate in increasing numbers from January through the late fall. When wild horses from the Pryor Mountains were examined, they were ovulating only from late March through early July. In other words, their season of ovulation, even when fed high-quality forage, was limited and substantially more compressed than that of domestic mares. After very little thought, this made sense. The climatic conditions of the Pryor Mountains are harsh, and foals born too early in the year would perish in the spring snows. Those born too late in the season would have little chance of surviving the coming winter. Thus, the compressed season of ovulation among these wild horses limited breeding to a period of time that assured that births occur at a time of the year when foals stood

the best chance of surviving. Even more interesting is that, as a rule, the older the wild horse herd, the more compressed the breeding season, thus implying that natural selection is removing the characteristic of a long breeding season from wild horses. The breeding season for deer, elk, and bison is very compressed, occurring in the late summer or fall. Their relatively short gestation periods of 200 to 270 days results in the young being born in April and May. Wild horses have a relatively long gestation period of 340 days, thus the foals are born in April and May also.

The approach of the breeding season for wild horses brings about significant changes in behaviors—particularly those of the stallion. He becomes more attentive to his mares, increasingly herding them so that none wanders from the band. The distance between mares will decrease substantially as the breeding season approaches. The stallion tolerates no other bands or stallions, reacting quickly and aggressively to protect his herd. In many cases he will take over band leadership from one of the mares to control the daily activities.

Before the first mare has come into estrus, the stallion is well aware that something is changing. Stallions, too, are seasonal breeders and their own internal clocks, which are also cued to day length, begin triggering important changes in physiology and behavior. Physiologically, the stallion is producing greater quantities of (below) Horses are almost unique among mammals in that the breeding season coincides with the birthing season. Gestation is approximately 340 days and it is often common for mares to have a "foal heat" and breed seven to ten days after the birth of a foal. (right) A receptive mare ready to breed will raise her tail to signal the stallion—he is always alert for these signals.

testosterone, and his aggressive behaviors are a reflection of this event. Among bands with more than one mature stallion, the dominant one now asserts himself, and it is almost always this dominant male who will ultimately carry out breeding. Despite his vigilance, stallions from within and without the band may breed with some of the mares. In some western herds up to 15% of pregnancies will be caused by other than the dominant stallion.

More than a month before a mare's first estrus cycle of the year, eggs begin to mature in her ovaries. At the same time, her estrogens (the female sex hormones) increase in her blood and urine. These first eggs stop maturing and degenerate. A second egg cycle will begin, followed by another increase in estrogens. This phenomenon will repeat itself several times during the months immediately preceding the onset of breeding activity, and it is referred to as the transitional season. The mares excrete estrogen in their urine and feces, providing an important cue for the stallions. During fall and winter, a mare's urination or defecation will go unnoticed by the stallion. That all changes as the breeding season nears. A typical stallion response will be to walk over to sniff the site of elimination. He may then display flehmen, which is a behavior associated with olfaction. This involves stretching his neck, raising his head, and rolling his lips upward and back toward his nostrils, where he "smells" whatever it was he touched with his lips. The flehmen is sometimes confused with a yawn—they do look similar. Following flehmen, which is a common behavior of many other

ungulates and carnivores, the stallion will defecate and/or urinate on the mare's elimination. It has been hypothesized that this controlled elimination by the stallion, known commonly as elimination marking behavior, is an olfactory message to any other males, which provides information about the social or sexual status of the stallion who possesses that mare. Mares do not display elimination marking behavior, and stallions do not display this behavior in response to eliminations from either immature males or immature females in the band.

Finally, sometime in April, the mare matures an egg and ovulates. As the mare approaches the time of ovulation, her estrogen concentrations reach their highest levels. She becomes sexually receptive to the stallion. Her behaviors change dramatically. She will become more active and eat less, and it is not unusual for her to become aggressive toward other mares in the band. The estrous mare will urinate frequently, usually in little squirts, and she will display a lot of tail-raising. This latter action exposes the vulva, and she will evert the clitoris rhythmically in a well-known action described as "winking." At some point in her estrus, usually two days before ovulation, she will begin to permit the stallion to mount her. By this time the stallion is paying intense attention to the estrous mare, nuzzling her, nickering, investigating her genital area, and displaying flehmen. Mutual grooming is a very important aspect of wild horse courtship. Finally, the mare will take a very rigid stance and permit the stallion to mount her, during which time she will turn her ears back and let her lips sag loosely. In extreme cases, estrous mares will actually seek out stallions.

It is always fun, but not scientifically wise, to look for the parallels between wild horse and human behaviors. I have imagined many parallels, but none is so dramatic or thought provoking as the notion of jealousy among horses. Dominant mares who are not in estrus often drive subordinate estrous mares away from the stallion to prevent breeding. What is going on here? Do wild horses experience jealousy? Perhaps not, but this behavior is uncomfortably close to our definition of the word.

All these behaviors are in contrast to an anestrous mare, one that is not maturing an ovum or ovulating and therefore not producing very high concentrations of estrogens. Stallions will approach all mares during the breeding season, in order to "test" their receptiveness. If an anestrous mare is approached aggressively by the stallion, she will flatten her ears, kick with her front and hind legs, and let out a high-pitched squeal that even the unpracticed ear can interpret as a sound of protest. Observation of wild horses during the breeding season and the information gained must be viewed with caution. Often, during the transition periods preceding and following the true breeding season, mares will display behavioral estrus but will not be ovulating. This is very common during the late summer and fall.

If a mare fails to become pregnant, she may pass through another estrous cycle and ovulate about 21 days later. A "regular" mare would continue these 21-day estrous cycles until she became pregnant or the breeding season ended, but it is clear that wild horses are not very regular. Some will not ovulate at all, others will ovulate only once a season, and some will ovulate several times in a season. It is very common for wild mares to have alternate-year breeding patterns. The most common cause of this pattern is something called lactational anestrus. A mare with a foal will continue to lactate as long as the foal nurses—among wild horses, foals will often nurse a full year, sometimes two, and on occasion young animals will nurse for three years. During this time, lactation's tremendous energy drain prevents the mare from ovulating.

A dramatic example of this phenomenon is seen among the two wild horse populations inhabiting Assateague Island. The horses inhabiting the Virginia portion of the island are gathered each July and the foals are sold in an auction. The mares are then returned to the island, where approximately 75% of them will become pregnant and produce new foals next year. The wild horses inhabiting the Maryland portion of the island are unmanaged, and a mare with a foal is stuck with the foal for as long as she will permit. It is very unusual to find a yearling that is not still nursing.

In contrast to the ones on the Virginia section, only about 45% of the mares on the Maryland portion of Assateague will produce foals on any given year. The majority of the Maryland mares that have been lactating all winter and spring are unable to come into estrus and ovulate. These particular wild horses have fewer foals because of the strain caused by long periods of lactation. This probably increases the survival rates of foals and surely helps preserve the overall condition of the mare during her lifetime. However, pregnancy rates among wild horses from Nevada, Oregon, and Wyoming do not seem to be influenced by lactational anestrus. These differences point to an important lesson here for those who would manage wild horses. Removing the very young animals preferred for adoption from wild horse herds also removes the stress of lactation from mares. Rather than controlling a herd's population, this practice may actually increase the foaling rates of mares left behind on the range.

At about day 35 of the pregnancy, the mare will produce extremely large quantities of estrogens, which first results in the pregnant mare again demonstrating behavioral estrus. Fortunately for those of us who study wild horses, this estrogen concentration is measurable in urine or fecal samples collected off the ground, allowing us to accurately diagnose pregnancy. This has allowed us to learn much about wild horse reproduction.

Until recently, no one knew very much about the success rate of wild horse pregnancies. Using these remote pregnancy diagnosis techniques, pregnancy loss has

Among wild horses, such as these on Assateague Island, it is not unusual for two- and even three-year-olds to remain with their mother. This often prevents the mare from reproducing on consecutive years.

As the time for the birth of her foal approaches, the mare leaves the band to find a hidden spot for the birth. Often she doesn't return to the band for several days. There are exceptions to every rule, and in one Wyoming herd, the mares simply lie down next to the band to foal.

been investigated among Pryor Mountain, Assateague Island, and Sable Island wild horses. Overall fetal loss rates were found to be as high as 25% and were age-dependent. The fetal loss rate among yearlings was 70% and dropped to about 5% in four-year-olds. We now understand the significant role of fetal loss in regulating foaling rates among wild horses.

Can we predict, with any accuracy, which mares in a herd or band will produce foals? As we have seen, mares not nursing foals come into estrus, ovulate, and become pregnant more often. Second, the age of a mare can help us predict her reproductive success. Young mares, the two- and three-year-olds, have low pregnancy rates, a high rate of fetal loss, and a low rate of live foals born. Mares between the ages of four and twelve get pregnant more often, lose few fetuses, and are highly successful at producing live foals. After about age fifteen, fertility decreases.

As with all things having to do with wild horses, reproductive rates vary widely across different ranges. Collectively, the pregnancy rates of wild mares from Nevada are about 57%, while that of wild mares from Wyoming are closer to 80%, and we have already seen the dramatic differences between closely related wild horses living on two different sections of Assateague Island. Nutrition plays an important role, too, both between and within herds. In the Granite Range, wild horse bands feeding on low-quality forage had lower reproductive rates than bands on higher-quality forage.

Foals are born about 340 days after conception, which means births for wild horses occur mostly in April and May. So compressed is the breeding season that close to 80% of foals among North American wild horses are born during these two months. As the time of parturition nears, the mare will begin to separate herself from the band, and finally she will wander off to have her foal in some secret place. Few scientists studying wild horses have been privileged to witness a birth. The newborn foal's first perceptible acts are erection and movement of its ears. Soon it can lift its head and shift to lying on its stomach. After about an hour or two it will stand.

The mare will lick the foal during this time but the purposes are still obscure. Some believe it is an encouragement to stand, while others believe it is the mare's way of identifying her foal by means of odor. Soon after they are standing, foals begin to nurse. First-time mothers are sometimes uncooperative. In this case the foal will walk down one side of the mare, cross under her neck, and move back down the other side to the udder. This behavior is called "heading off" and more often than not will stimulate the mare to cooperate. Sometimes the foal will have trouble nursing and exhibit a behavior known as "pushing." This term hardly describes the almost violent poking of the foal's nose into the mare's udder, and it is not uncommon for the mare to become annoyed. If a foal becomes frustrated at nursing, it will paw at the ground and even kick the mother. In order to help the foal, the mare may plant her back legs and step forward with the front legs, to expose her udder.

During the first two months of life, male foals will spend up to 40% more time nursing than females. This interesting phenomenon also occurs in other ungulate species. A greater investment in males by the mother has, at least in theory, genetic benefits. It has been suggested that the weight of a male animal at the time of weaning depends upon the amount of time it has nursed, and it is factual that heavier weights at the time of weaning lead to heavier adult weights. In turn, larger, heavier stallions have an advantage in fighting rivals to obtain mares. Finally, a stallion, because he breeds with many mares, passes on more DNA to future generations than a mare. It is only a theoretical construct, but it may explain why mares spend more effort nursing males than females.

While the mare's bond to the foal is very strong, the foal's bond to its mother is initially weak. It will take two to three days for the foal to form a strong bond with its mother. During those few days the mare will chase any other horses away, even last year's offspring, in order to prevent any confusion in the bonding process. For the first week, the mare will take the responsibility for keeping track of the foal, but after that it becomes the foal's responsibility to follow her. Once a strong bond has been established in the foal, the mare will permit other horses to investigate the young animal and even touch it. Occasionally old mares beyond their own reproductive years will bond to a new foal and even try to protect it.

Sometime during their first week of life foals will begin to graze, but their efforts are clumsy. They still lack the coordination to walk and graze at the same time, in the manner of the adults. How soon a wild foal learns to graze is dependent upon watching its mother and other horses in the band. For its first month the foal will eat some of its mother's feces, too, and in this way obtain important bacteria necessary for digestion of grasses.

The foal has a special place in the harem band social order. After the first week foals become extremely social, investigating everything about them, including other horses in the band. Play behavior begins immediately and is usually conducted alone. Foals run in circles, kicking their heels, developing skills that could be important if the herd is forced to flee some threat. Male foals play more often and more aggressively than females. By about four weeks of age, the foals begin to act out play-fights together. They kick, rear up with one another, and bite, but without true aggression. Foals do not quickly develop dominance hierarchies, either. As with the young of most species, foals show great curiosity, and they not only find other foals of great interest but the young of other species as well. I have witnessed foals attempting to play with crows, ravens, and even sika deer fawns, a species of Asian elk found on Assateague Island. The adult crows and ravens showed little interest in reciprocating, but the sika deer fawn was clearly as intrigued with the foal as the foal was with the fawn. They spent considerable time cautiously approaching one another, testing the wind, looking back at their respective mothers for reassurance (who generally ignored the youngsters), and finally stretching out their necks and touching noses. The innocence of youth truly extends to our wild creatures.

On Assateague I administered contraceptive drugs to mares with the use of a blowgun. Because this tool is so silent, I was once able to dart three mares from my position as I sat quietly in the marsh. Apparently they thought the dart was little more than an oversized mosquito. Between each darting, I had to set the blowgun aside for

(left) Male foals, such as this new Pryor Mountain colt, spend more time nursing than females. In order to become a dominant and strong harem stallion one day, the male foal must have a good start in life. The rewards are increased genetic contributions to the herd in later years. (below) Foals are extremely curious and this new foal makes an early acquaintance with her yearling sister.

several minutes while preparing a new dart. As I completed that task I reached for the blowgun, only to find it was gone. I felt around in the grass behind me, sure that it must be where I had set it down. As I turned I spotted a mischievous foal only a few months old. From the foal's mouth the blowgun dangled as the curious little horse chewed intently on the rubber mouthpiece. I chuckled at the inquisitiveness of this foal, which is typical of the species.

Ungulates demonstrate two strategies for the survival of the very young of the species. Some, like deer, are classified as "hiders"—the fawn remains hidden by itself for long periods of time while the mother forages. She will visit her fawn, or fawns, several times during the day. The wild horse on the other hand, is a "follower," in which there is constant and close contact between the mother and the offspring. This strategy is common to species of the open plains and is another hint of the habitat type upon which the horse evolved. Whereas "hiders" remain motionless when faced with danger, foals— because they are followers—need the ability to run soon after birth. To facilitate this, the horse's fetus is extremely active from the third month of gestation and is born with

remarkably good muscle tone. Because of this, young horses soon learn to run with agility and speed.

The horse is unique among large mammals in that the season of birth coincides with the breeding season. This has led to a fascinating reproductive phenomenon known as postpartum estrus or the "foal heat." Seven to ten days following the birth of a foal, mares will often return to estrus, ovulate, and become pregnant again. The success rate of these pregnancies is not very high among wild horses. However, we know very little about the causes of the low success. Conceptions may be higher than we think, but early pregnancy loss, which we cannot measure in wild horses, may be very high. A small amount of data exists that suggests that mares producing new eggs during foal heat are unsuccessful at releasing these ova.

Reproductive success of wild horses is often measured by the production of live foals but, in reality, reproductive success is achieved only when a foal itself has grown to reproduce. The first year of a foal's life is perilous, and the odds are high that it may not see its first birthday. Of all the age classes within a herd, mortality is highest for foals. It is estimated that 20% to 25% of wild foals die within a year of their birth. This may be a valid

If more than one foal is born in a band, they will quickly find one another and spend considerable time together. Young wild horses with others of the same or close age in their band will tend to stay in their band longer than horses without age peers.

generalization, but foal survival will actually range from 0% to 100% on different ranges and under different weather conditions. In 1976, I noted a 100% foal survival among the Pryor Mountain horses after a mild winter. Yet a year and a bitter winter later, not a single foal survived. The same degree of variability was found among foals born on other horse ranges. Whatever the causes of foal mortality, there is an inverse relationship between the number of foals born in a given year and the survival rates of the foals. It is likely that during years with low birth rates, there has been a great deal of fetal and undetected neonatal loss, particularly among fetuses and newborn that were too weak to survive anyway.

Another potential peril for foals comes from the takeover of the band by a new stallion. When this happens, there is often aggressive action by the new stallion directed toward foals, and on rare occasions the new stallion will kill foals soon after he takes over the band. Foal killing has been documented in the North American wild horses and among the Camargue wild horses of France. In all reported cases, the foals that were killed were not the offspring of the offending stallion. This behavior is very interesting and has also been witnessed in other species, including some nonhuman primates, African lions, and bears. This behavior implies that the stallion wants to rid the band of young horses that do not carry his own DNA. At the same time, the death of the foal causes its mother to quit lactating and stimulates early estrus, making her available to the new stallion for breeding. In this manner the new stallion not only has eliminated a competitor's genes, but he has passed his own DNA to a successive generation.

The aggression of the new stallion is even greater if the foal is a male. This was brought home to me in the fall of 1989, when an epidemic of equine encephalitis killed several horses on Assateague Island. A five-month-old male foal was orphaned, and although he was old enough to fend for himself nutritionally, he wandered about the island attempting to join other bands, driven by that gregarious equine nature. Each attempt was met with extreme aggression by the band stallions, none of whom were his father (his father died from the disease, too), and on several occasions it was clear that the stallion would have killed the foal if it had persisted. The foal was covered with bites and on one occasion the stallion drove the young animal well out into Sinepuxent Bay. The story had a happy ending—in the fall, after many long and lonely nights, the foal wandered into a bachelor band and took up peaceful residence with them. By the following spring the little male carried out mutual grooming with his much larger adult bachelor companions. Two other foals orphaned that same year were females, and both were permitted to join new bands during that fall, without undue attention by the stallions.

In most species of wildlife, reproductive success requires genetic diversity among the population. For example, populations of zoo animals must be constantly manipulated, with males and females moved to and from other zoos to maintain sufficient genetic diversity for successful reproduction. This has been a concern for wild horses—particularly for those herds that are small and relatively confined.

Many years ago I watched with some fascination as government employees expressed their concerns about the Pryor Mountain horses. This population consists of about 100 to 150 horses living on approximately 45,000 acres. The Pryor horses have been around for a long time, perhaps 200 years or more, and they are small-bodied animals, weighing about 600 to 700 pounds. They have small ears and colors are restricted to black, sorrel, buckskin, dun, and grulla. There are no white horses or pintos and only an occasional palomino.

Many smaller wild horse herds are genetically inbred, but few herds have any serious problems from this inbreeding. Improving the bloodlines of wild horse herds is best left to wild horses.

Many of the personnel in charge of wild horses are themselves "horse people" who own and breed horses, and their views of the wild horse often carry with them the biases of modern horse breeders. In the Pryors, there were complaints of size (too small), ears (too small), colors (too few), and poor conformation (not like a quarter horse), all thought to be caused by inbreeding. Before too long, there were proposals to introduce horses from Wyoming, to "improve" the blood line. Concerned that a potentially old and unique population of wild horses might be genetically destroyed by a well-meant but ill-advised move, I employed the aid of a well-known wildlife geneticist from one of the world's major zoos. As we sat around the wood stove in a Pryor Mountain log cabin, he patiently listened to the concerns of the wranglers. Finally, he asked two questions: Are the Pryor horses reproducing as well as other wild horses? Are the foals surviving to sexual maturity with the same degree of success as that of other herds? The answer to both questions was yes. The geneticist explained that while the Pryor Mountain horses might be inbred (which has since been proven to be true), they are not experiencing inbreeding problems. The only things that are really important to wild horses—the ability to reproduce and survival of the young—were going well. He advised that the horses be left alone.

Many wild horse herds are in fact inbred, but it is clear that this inbreeding has not caused problems. Horses have an exceptional ability to overcome genetic bottlenecks. In order to register a thoroughbred, one must be able to trace the animal's ancestry to one of three stallions—the Goldolfin Barb, the Byerly Turk, or the Darley Arabian. That is a real genetic bottleneck, yet thoroughbreds are doing reasonably well. And the 1,000 Przewalski's horses alive today came through a genetic bottleneck of 13 animals. Thus, horses somehow manage a degree of inbreeding that might harm other species.

Despite that biological ability, wild horses also have an innate behavioral mechanism that reduces the amount of inbreeding within a herd. The highly developed social organization of the harem band would, at first glance, lead one to think that daughters could be bred by fathers—or by brothers in multiple stallion bands. But as we have already seen, young mares have a tendency to leave the band before they are bred. When actual degrees of inbreeding were calculated for wild horses of the Camargue in France and on several different ranges in North America, they were less than one-half of what was expected if all breeding had occurred randomly. On Assateague Island, 20 of 28 mares born during an

eight-year period left their natal band before reaching sexual maturity. From the eight mares that remained with their father's bands, only five foals were born during a period of time when 22 foals would have been possible, for a 22.7% foaling rate. Of the 20 mares who moved to new bands, nine were with stallions who were half-brothers, and those mares produced only seven foals during a period of time when 19 were possible, for a 36.8% foaling rate. Eleven other mares who lived in bands with unrelated stallions produced 21 foals over a period of time when 34 foals could have been born, for a foaling rate of 61.8%. This dispersal mechanism thus reduces inbreeding. The low foaling rate among mares who remained with their fathers or moved to their half-brothers is very interesting.

In addition to the young mares leaving their natal band, stallions appear to avoid their daughters when the latter do not leave. At least three different investigators have documented the fact that Pryor Mountain stallions almost never breed their daughters even if they stay within the band, and only a single incidence of a stallion breeding a daughter was witnessed among the Sable Island wild horses. Some degree of familiarity in the stallion's memory significantly reduces inbreeding within a herd.

At least six factors must be considered in the reproductive biology of the wild horse if we are to understand both the success and the variability seen across North America and the world. First, genetics provides a foundation from which to examine any variation in reproductive success. Horses with older genetic origins—that is, more primitive types—may be assumed to have taken less time to become adjusted to their harsh environments than those with more recent historic origins. Second, habitats and other environmental factors will drive the process of natural selection, and the more hostile the environment, the more dramatic the changes in the biology of the horse. Third, the greater the length of time any given population of horses has been living in its environment, the longer the process of natural selection can be assumed to have worked its biological magic. Finally, three other factors affect reproductive success. Changes in population densities, age-class profiles, and sex ratios—whether caused by man through roundups and removals or by nature—have brought about rapid changes in the reproductive biology of the wild horse.

Regardless of the forces, it is clear that the wild horse can reproduce successfully enough to thrive in most places in this world.

SEASONS AND SIGNALS

The bay stallion was grazing in one of Assateague's many marshes. I watched as he ambled along, tearing at tufts of grass, shaking his head and swishing his tail. There was nothing particularly distinctive about this horse, except that he seemed to live a particularly lonely life for one so young. Such a young stallion should have been with a bachelor group, or with a mare, but to the best of the knowledge of those of us who studied these horses, this bay had never been with either. Mostly he lived a solitary life near Pine Tree Campground, from which he earned the name Pine Tree Bay.

Something about Pine Tree Bay did seem different this day. Horses are almost always cautiously alert, marking you far off and early with their tremendous eyesight. Even if they don't see you, they'll generally hear a trespasser and so wander off long before you get near. But Pine Tree Bay seemed singularly unaware of me as I struggled toward him from the rear through the thick, noisy marsh.

Not until I was very near did the horse sense I was there, and when he did, we both jumped, startled. The horse was understandably surprised by how near I was, and I was shocked by how easy it had been. The marsh is a difficult place to stalk any wild creature.

The next time I had the occasion to approach him I tried again to sneak very near. It worked. With the horse unaware of me, I loudly clapped my hands. Pine Tree Bay kept right on grazing. It was then I realized that this horse was deaf. And I wondered, did his long, lonely life have anything to do with his deafness? A young and healthy horse, Pine Tree Bay should have been in the company of others. Was his deafness preventing him from communicating with other horses, keeping him from socializing?

Perhaps so. Yet as I write this book I'm happy to report that the Pine Tree Bay has found company with the pretty sorrel mare Patty and her yearling. After his years of loneliness, the Pine Tree Bay is finally in the company of his kind.

A s seasons change, so do the lives of wild horses, although the degree of change will depend upon the particular location of the herd. Horses living far to the south—where temperatures change little and food and water are always available—change habits less than those living in mountain environments or in more northerly latitudes. But, regardless of the location, the same adaptability that characterizes every other aspect of the wild horse also guides them through yearly seasonal changes.

In order to understand how seasons affect wild horses, it might be helpful to examine two herds in different locations. Let us examine the yearly rhythms of the Pryor Mountain wild horses. Their range varies from desert at the lowest elevations, to heights of 9,000 feet. Sweltering summer temperatures can exceed 115 degrees and winter temperatures can drop to minus-45 degrees. We will also look at the seasonal changes in behaviors and habits among the barrier island horses of Assateague Island, where fierce fall storms and damp cold winter weather contrast with balmy springs and insect-laden summers.

Summers in the Pryor Mountains of southcentral Montana are relatively good times for the 130 or so wild horses living there, despite some difficult dry conditions at lower elevations where temperatures get extremely hot and grass is scarce. Lying in the rain shadow of the Absoraka Mountains, these lower desert portions get only about seven inches of rain a year. As the snows of winter recede, the horses begin their climb up through the rocky terrain of scrub juniper and mountain mahogany, emerging on the edges of the high timbered slopes. Here the plentiful grasses, cooler temperatures, water from melting snowfields, and fewer insects make life easier for these tough horses.

By mid-July the breeding season is over. Stallions relax and the bands return to a less hectic life. Everyone focuses on eating. The stallions begin to fatten up on the good grass and gain back some of the weight they lost during the "horse wars" of the breeding season. Although they still sleep and play a lot, the foals are old enough to follow the band, and they rapidly learn its rhythms and necessary social behaviors. As the sun warms the timbered slopes, many members of the band lie down for periods of up to an hour, guarded by the one member that remains standing and alert.

It is a time when communication skills are being honed. A mare nickers to her foal to get up off the ground. The foal nickers in response and whenever it returns to its mother. These are the same nickers that stallions use when courting a mare, and this form of communication probably represents quiet "talk" for wild horses. The foal also learns the meaning of the whinny. Enthusiastically exploring, foals often wander far from their mare. A robust whinny from the concerned mare brings the foal galloping back, or at the very least elicits a return whinny from the foal, betraying its location. The whinny, when used in this context, is therefore something of a mild, long-range distress call. Wild horses can clearly recognize an individual's whinnies, allowing them to communicate without actually seeing one another. The neigh is a special call that stallions use to call back a foal that has wandered too near another band. In addition, horses can also tell one another apart by sight.

Wild horses are skilled at finding grass even in dry desert country. These Pryor Mountain horses summer in this high mountain country. During the winter they merely get by on the lower but warmer portions of the range where little grass is found.

(below) As long as water from melting snowfields is available, the horses are at home in the high timbered slopes. Cooler temperatures also keep insects at a minimum. (right) As a yearling naps, her mother stands watch in the high elevations of the Pryor Mountains. There are few threats to horses here, but they remain alert nonetheless.

I have always been amazed when a wild horse identifies another horse by sight alone, even though the one being identified has no apparent markings.

Sense of smell is important to communication between wild horses. When greeting one another, two horses will often touch nostrils and sniff with great energy, presumably to identify each other. We have already seen earlier how the odors of urine and feces from mares appear to be a form of communication. Olfaction becomes very important around the water sources, and bands will spend several minutes sniffing the air downwind before approaching a water hole, to determine if horses outside their own group are nearby.

Summer days pass lazily for Pryor wild horses. Only the daily trip for water interrupts rhythmic bouts of grazing and sleeping, and these trips are short because of

(above) Olfaction is a very important communication behavior among horses. Here, a young mare reassures herself of the bond with her mother. (right) Wild horses commonly roll in the dust to relieve themselves of insects. Often this behavior is contagious, and a whole band will soon follow. Each band has a favorite dusting area.

the ample drinking water and lush grasses resulting from melting snow. The horses enjoy both the cool, high-elevation temperatures and the fact that this coolness keeps insects to a minimum.

The summer life of the Assateague wild horses is not so idyllic. Insects during the summer make life truly miserable for these horses, spurring movements from winter home ranges in the marsh to areas of the island with fewer insects. The swamps of this barrier island harbor an impressive array of insects including dog ticks, deer ticks (complete with Lyme disease), and swarming clouds of gnats. But it is the mosquitoes and green-headed flies that agonize the horses. One of the great ironies of Assateague Island is that during wet summers when the flies are not numerous, the mosquitoes hatch in great numbers, and during dry summers when the mosquitoes are tolerable, the green-headed flies emerge in profusion. I can't be sure, but I believe the serious and painful fly bites cause far more problems for the horses than the mosquitoes.

During dry summers the horses flee the marsh for the breezy interdune areas, which are rolling, sparsely vegetated sand dunes inland from the beach. Finally the horses move to the beaches themselves. They leave the rich grasses of the bay-side marshes to scour the sand dunes for beach grass and sea oats, all in an effort to seek the sea breezes and the little protection they offer from biting insects. When insects are particularly bad, the horses immerse themselves in the ocean during the hottest hours, sometimes with only their heads above water. The horses would rather be jostled and beat by the waves than face the tortuous insects.

I have often seen bands of Assateague horses running wildly about, with no particular destination, as if to run away from the annoying creatures. On very bad insect years, the bands of horses will begin impressive migrations up and down the island, moving up to 10 miles from their winter home ranges. The northern eight miles of Assateague Island have fewer swamps and dunes. Many horses choose to spend the entire summer in this region of frequent breezes and few insects. To do so requires the merging bands to show more tolerance as the distance between bands decreases. With the insects as a common enemy, the horses seem to forget some of the animosities of the previous spring. Summer is not a good time for these animals.

A great deal of time is spent rolling furiously about on their backs in the sand, relieving themselves of the itching caused by the insects. This activity may go on for many minutes. When I've examined these sites after the horses have moved, I've found them littered with the carcasses of insects. Western wild horses similarly roll in dust to relieve themselves of insects.

Fall in the Pryor Mountains is a truly wonderful time—for man and beast. The horses enjoy cooler temperatures and the cured, protein-rich grasses of the upper elevations, although their search for water becomes more difficult. The daily routine continues much as during the summer months, but the journeys to water are now longer.

(left) A young Assateague Island stallion grazes marsh grass during the insect-free days of autumn. This is a relaxed time for barrier island horses who are recovering from a summer of mosquitoes and biting flies. (below) Winter in the mountains can sometimes be pleasant. During milder years, limited snow permits access to food, and temperatures can be quite moderate.

The horses now find water in seeps, small springs, and even several old abandoned mines, until the coming of the first snows. These journeys take the horses to progressively lower elevations, where they encounter other bands. More time is spent testing the air before moving in to water, and any sign of other horses or potential predators results in loud blowing and wheezing snorts of alarm. Blowing seems infectious. Once the stallion has snorted his alarm, others in the band do the same, until all are snorting and blowing, making a tremendous racket.

As bands begin to cross paths in the fall, one of the most poorly understood stallion behaviors becomes apparent. Wherever there are wild horses, there are numerous large mounds of feces, better known as stud piles. No one knows exactly why a pile site is chosen, but once a stud pile has been built, no stallion will pass by without contributing to the heap. Mares rarely defecate on these piles, implying this is an evolutionary trait common only to the males. Some piles are impressive in their size, and it is apparent when a pile is "in use" and when it is old.

Theories abound regarding the purpose of stud piles. One has it that this is a lost or vestigial behavior that originated when horses were still territorial and that they actually mark boundaries. The problem with that theory is that most stud piles are within home ranges and not on the boundaries themselves. Another theory is that these piles are location markers and help horses know where the band is located. Still another theory is that they help wild horse bands avoid one another. In other words, if you come upon a fresh stud pile it might be better to move on, but if you find an old unused pile the surrounding area is safe to use. Whatever the purpose of these deposits, they are a common part of wild horse habitat.

Fall on Assateague Island begins to bring relief to the harried horses. As temperatures cool and the insects become fewer, the horses head for their winter home ranges with unerring accuracy. The north end of the island quickly empties of its equine vacationers. Those horses that resided for the summer in the state park, where managers spray to control mosquitoes and flies, head back to the marshes. The diets of the horses once again become predominantly marsh grasses, and each band settles down in a familiar setting.

Having found their places in the band hierarchy among other foals, one- and two-year-olds, and the mares, each foal now establishes a relationship with their stallion. Foals and stallions exhibit a striking form of communication called tooth clapping or snapping. As a foal with extended and exposed neck approaches a stallion, it will roll back its lips, expose its teeth, and clack them in the stallion's face. While female foals demonstrate this behavior to both adult mares and stallions, male foals most often display this behavior to the stallion. Stallions often act aggressively toward foals before this display but seldom afterwards. Some believe this to be a signal from the foal that it recognizes the adult's dominance, particularly that of the stallion, which would explain why the stallion ceases to act aggressively. Others contend that this behavior is some sort of substitute activity for nursing.

Once the foal has displayed snapping and has indicated its subordinate position, some stallions appear to merely ignore the energetic young horses. Other stallion-foal relationships are much closer. Hot Air Balloon, the legendary Assateague stallion I mentioned earlier, was a volatile animal who frequently picked, and lost, fights with other stallions. But as a father, Hot Air Balloon had few peers. He would spend endless hours neck wrestling with his foals, even occasionally engaging in rough and tumble wrestling on his knees.

In autumn the island horses face the deadly prospect of hurricanes. However, the Assateague horses have lived with these storms for 320 years. With one notable exception, which I will discuss in the next chapter, there is no evidence that their survival was ever really threatened. They have learned to move into the thickest stands of pine, greenbrier, reedlike phragmites, and shrubs when the winds reach 60 or 70 miles per hour. Often they will lie down during the worst of the storm. At worst, hurricanes appear to be a temporary inconvenience.

By November the insects are completely gone, the horses are once again alone on the marshes, temperatures have cooled down, and life is relatively tranquil. It is a time of quiet repose for the island horses.

Winter in the Pryor Mountains is like a toss of the dice. I have seen winters there with temperatures as low as minus-45 degrees and snow up to the horses' bellies, and there have been others where the days were cool at worst and snow was almost absent. As snow accumulates at the higher elevations, the horses move south and down the slopes into areas where the grass and water grow scarce. These wild horses really face a dilemma with the coming of harsh weather. To stay up high where the grass is better would mean facing strength-sapping cold temperatures and snow. But should they go too low in their escape, they will face the desertlike sands and run out of grass. Finally, if the snows and cold follow them to the bottom of the range, their dilemma becomes a disaster.

The horses adopt two behaviors to battle the cold and snow. First, they conserve energy by spending hours standing absolutely still. Second, when conditions are favorable, the horses will seek grass on high, wind-swept ridges kept free of snow. Since deep, calm snow is very dangerous to the horses, the wind that blows it away can be their friend.

(below) A soaked barrier island horse pays little attention to the rain. Of all the adverse elements, these horses seem to dislike high winds the most. (right) Lactating mares face the greatest dangers on western wild horse ranges during the winter. With demands of a new foal, the production of milk robs the mare of calories, making survival even more difficult. This mare survived the winter, but she is gaunt and in poor condition.

The young Assateague stallion, "Dagger," relaxes in the thick underbrush of the island. At age seven, he has yet to acquire his first band. His mother was one of the first mares on the island to be treated with a contraceptive vaccine, and if she had been treated a year earlier, Dagger wouldn't be here.

During the winter, members of the band wander farther afield without the stallion's interference. More young females disperse during this season than at any other time of the year. The elimination marking behavior of the stallions, also noted earlier, disappears during the winter months, presumably because the urine and feces of the mares no longer contain the chemical signals that elicited this behavior during the breeding season. It may also have to do with the lowered testosterone levels of the stallion. He may just not be as interested in mares.

As the snows deepen and grasses become even harder to find, the horses will turn to whatever forage can be found above the snow, eating shrubs, small trees, and almost anything that's edible and available. If the winter is severe enough, some foals, yearlings, and even adults will begin eating old fecal piles, extracting whatever nutrition they can from the poorly digested material. Lactating mares become perilously thin and foals face the most dangerous weeks of their lives. Now the dominant-subordinate relationships between mares take on monumental importance and life itself is at stake. The dominant mares get the best of what little food is available and the subordinate mares get less. As it has always been, only the strongest will survive. The only thing the Pryor horses can do is wait for spring's lifesaving grasses.

On Assateague, the tables have been turned. While the Pryor horses thrived on summer grasses, the Assateague horses suffered through the worst time of their year. Now, in the heart of winter, while the Pryor horses work to survive the winter cold and snow, the Assateague horses move through the winter with relative ease. Bitter, wet northeastern storms buffet the coast and the horses, but still they find life easier than during the summer. Occasionally it gets cold enough for the bay to freeze, but it seems to have little effect on the horses because of their shaggy, thick coats. Nor have I seen rain or even the rare snows that occasionally blanket the island bother the horses unduly. Even when several feet of snow once covered the island for several days, the horses easily pawed down to the thick, plentiful marsh grass.

If there is one facet of the weather that does bother them it is the wind. The marshes are interspersed with loblolly pine forests and, as the winter winds increase, the horses seek shelter in the lee of these windbreaks. Despite the thick vegetation on this island, I can often quickly locate bands in the winter by simply figuring out where the horses would go to find the greatest shelter from the wind. During one particularly fierce winter storm, a mare and her foal sought a rather cozy shelter under the porch of an abandoned National Park ranger station. They remained there for two days, nibbling away at the sparse beach grass that grew at the edges, saving body heat by avoiding the wind.

One of the most interesting behaviors exhibited by the Assateague horses during the winter is their obvious perception of and reaction to humans. The rare human incursion onto the marshes at this time of the year causes moderate alarm and increased alertness among the horses. These animals are used to seeing people on the beaches or the interdune area. But few humans venture into the marshes at any time of the year and practically none cross these grassy plains in the winter. When people approach a wintering band while on the marsh, the horses usually move to some new grazing area. Approach the same horses a day later in the interdune areas, and they will not be alarmed. Accustomed to seeing humans hiking on these dunes, the horses understand that people "belong" there. In the Pryor Mountains, most horses can be approached to within 100 yards or so on foot. But because they are rounded up every few years by men on horseback, a human on horseback sets them "off to the races" with great alarm. Thus, events have contexts in both time and space for the horses.

By March, the Assateague horses enter one of the most pleasant times of the year. The cold of winter has moderated, there are no insects, and food is still plentiful. They roam about their home ranges, rarely encountering other bands at close quarters, and generally appear to be enjoying this special time of the year. Foals are now almost yearlings and their individual personalities are emerging. The warming days bring forth a new energy in the young animals. They spend considerable time racing about the marsh and the dunes with no apparent motivation other than running for sheer pleasure. They have reached an age where they are bold enough to seek attention from adult animals and, if I may apply human terms, tease older animals with nudges and nips. Sometimes the scenes created by these energetic youthful horses are light and humorous. Several years ago, in March, I was watching a yearling race about its band, running into other animals, nipping at the flanks of some, and in general disturbing a peaceful time for the band on the marsh. The band stallion was becoming less and less tolerant of this frivolous behavior. The stallion, who was standing next to a large, deep tidal pool in the marsh, would periodically stop his grazing and stare at the young horse intently. Finally, as the yearling came speeding up alongside the stallion, the big male horse thrust his shoulder into the young horse with an action similar to a healthy block by a lineman. The young animal went sailing through the air into the pool, where he disappeared underwater. A second or two later he surfaced and stood quietly in the cold water, his exuberance a bit dampened. The old stallion just stood there staring at him and one can only wonder what horse emotions were running through his equine brain.

(right) "Out of the earth, I sing for them. A horse nation . . . I sing for them, the animals." Teton Sioux song. (below) A sleek stallion scratches his nose in the stillness of an alpine meadow.

While we tend to think of wild horses racing across open prairie, these highly adaptable animals are equally at home in saltwater marshes on barrier islands.

When spring returns, so do the urgencies of reproduction. The transitional ovarian season begins for the mares, triggering aggressive behavior in the stallions. Now the "horse wars" begin once again. Bachelor stallions begin to roam far and wide again, searching for mares. It is a time of opportunity for bachelors. Old harem stallions that have succumbed to the rigors of the winter have left entire bands without protection. The luckier bachelors will literally stumble across entire bands in need of a stallion, and others will find a few mares from bands that broke up after their stallion died. Still others will find single young mares that dispersed during the winter months.

Seasonal changes in the lives of wild horses living on other ranges also have a rhythm that reflects their environmental changes. In central Australia, at least half of the year is characterized by drought. During their summer months, horses are drawn in large numbers to dwindling water holes along the dry river bottoms. Home ranges shrink and interactions between bands become more frequent. Available grasses are quickly used up. Summer is the time of stress for Australian horses. As their winter approaches, the rains come—a relative thing in central Australia—filling up water holes and rivers. The horses can disperse to find new sources of grass. For the Australian brumbies, like the Assateague horses, winter is a friend.

In eastern Nevada both winter and summer conspire against the wild horses. Summer heat reduces the water and drives the horses together at the few remaining water holes, as in Australia, but winter brings frigid temperatures that rob the animals of calories. Deep snows often prevent the weakening animals from feeding adequately. The horses can disperse during the winter and cover much larger areas, thereby taking pressure off the sparse grass.

Seasons, and the environmental changes they bring, dictate the habits of practically every wild horse herd on earth. Winter is the best time of the year for some populations, and summer can bring untold miseries. Yet the opposite is true for other horse herds. Wherever it lives, the amazingly adaptable wild horse has evolved strategies to survive snow, insects, drought, rain, and an incredible range of temperature extremes. Through it all the wild horse not only survives but prospers in environments that would defeat less resilient species.

DEATH
AND PREDATION

Gray clouds scudded on a cold northeast wind, dragging an occasional mist from the ocean to the dunes. Despite the foreboding nature of the weather, I strolled through the sparse grasses of the hard dunes, wandering at will, enjoying the fine wildness of windy Assateague and relaxing after my day spent darting mares.

March is a cool and quiet time on the island, and since I'm often one of the first people to return after winter, I'm also often the first to see what winter has wrought. As I shuffled through the sand over the top of a dune, I came to an abrupt halt. There, in a shallow ravine, lay the remains of an old friend.

Among the dense bayberry, beneath a particularly tall shrub, was the desiccated corpse of the sorrel mare M4, the thin white stripe that marked her face still visible. I studied the site of her last hours and could see the depressions near her hooves, made when she vainly tried to rise one last time. It was some comfort to note that since the holes were shallow, she likely hadn't struggled long. She must have sought this spot behind the lee side of the tall dune to escape the frigid winter wind. Lying in the shadow of the shrubs she came to the end of her days, buffeted by the wind, losing a race with old age. M4 was 20 years old.

I clambered down to her side and ran my hand along the dry hide of her neck, something that no other human had done. I am a scientist, but my emotional self mourned her loss. During those moments of grief I failed to realize that I should have been celebrating her life, not mourning her death. M4 had been born wild and had lived untamed, racing the wind down wild and lovely shores. She had never been roped, captured, corralled, or otherwise handled and had come to the end of a long life beneath the sun and on the turf that had forever been her home.

I turned away from the horse and the indifferent wind. The walk home seemed particularly long that day.

Fertility control and mortality control are the two factors that work upon animals to balance populations with the carrying capacity of the habitat. Natural fertility control occurs among many wild animal populations, causing reproductive rates to lower as populations increase. We do not understand all the physiological mechanisms that lead to decreased reproductive success, but the logic of such an approach is undeniable.

Mortality is the most visible control on animal populations and the first one we think of when discussing the subject of wildlife population growth. Both affect wild horses.

The causes of mortality in wild horses are many. Horses succumb to old age (which in itself actually covers a lot of ground), foal mortality, nutritionally related death caused by poor climatic conditions, severe winters, disease, predation, and accidents. All of these factors play a role in the mortality rates of wild horses, but they vary in their relevance across the world. In general, natural mortality among wild horse populations, under the best of conditions, is probably about 5% to 10% annually, and we consider mortality rates among wild horses to be time-specific rather than age-specific. That is, extreme climatic conditions and differences in range quality can change these rates significantly, regardless of the age structure of the herd. A healthy, well-kept domestic horse may live for more than 30 years, but most of our wild horses around the world are lucky to make it to 20. For many wild horse populations, the average age of death may be 10 years or less.

Let's start exploring this subject with a spectacularly healthy stallion who makes it to 20. He will die eventually, but why? We have already noted that he will lose his harem band at some point in his life, and the stress that comes with living alone may lead to some disease that under less stressful conditions might not have been lethal. But what about the mares who make it to 20? Eventually they will die too—and perhaps the single greatest cause is worn teeth and progressively poorer nutrition. The teeth of wild horses slowly but surely grind away from eating grasses covered with sand and dirt, until the animal can no longer chew food sufficiently for digestion.

In 1992, I found the carcass of an Assateague stallion we knew as "T-Stallion." "T" was a legend because he had as many as 22 mares in his band at one time. He spent his years a few hundred yards out in the bay on small and brushy Tingle's Island. As he grew older, "T" was unable to defend his large band, until in his last five years he had but five mares. When he died, we believed him to be at least 26, which is ancient for an Assateague horse. It was disconcerting for me to find his body in the bay's backwater, as much as if I'd found the body of some human legend. Science prevailed and I steeled myself for an examination. I found that his teeth were virtually gone, ground down to the gums. In the months preceding his disappearance, I'd noted his weight loss and final emaciation. The speed of a horse is of no avail in a race with time. Although he had escaped all other forms of death, his teeth had let him down, and "T" shared the fate of most old wild horses. The skulls of many Pryor Mountain horses also show significant tooth wear.

Old age creeps up on wild horses. As the end nears, they become gaunt and thin, and even a moderate winter will test the survival of old animals. Few wild horses ever reach 20 years.

Even horses in good condition can fall prey to unusually hard winters. Extreme cold saps the animals of calories, and sparse forage is often buried under deep or crusted snow.

Thus, all other things being equal, wild horses living in areas where the soil is gritty or sandy will generally die younger than those living upon gentler soils.

Naturally, climatic conditions can aggravate poor nutritional conditions. Even well-conditioned horses with good teeth may not survive hard winters. Nearly half the Pryor Mountain horses died in the winter of 1977-78 when extreme cold and deep snow drove the animals down from the grassy higher elevations. There had been few winds to clean the snow from the ridges, and the snow grew too deep for the horses to paw down to the grass. Unfortunately for the horses, they found the snow equally deep on the normally desertlike lower elevations. Their fates were sealed. The horses stood belly deep in the snow until they could stand no longer, finally just lying down to die. Though grieved by what I had witnessed, I knew that the population would rebound. In only a few years the Pryor Mountain population was back to 130 animals.

Just who survives hard winters like the one I just described—and who doesn't? Not a single foal survived that winter. They were just too small, had too few reserves to fall back on, and were too weak to take on the elements. More lactating mares died that winter than nonlactating mares. That is hardly surprising either. Pregnancy represents a remarkably small caloric cost to a mare, but lactation is a killer. Even under the best of conditions, lactating wild mares are thin and gaunt, their fat stores used to produce nutritious milk. Adult mares that are not lactating fare better during severe winter weather, and the longer it has been since they last gave birth, the better are their chances of survival. Stallions fare better than most too. During the particularly cold December of 1992, I was involved in the capture of 500 eastern Nevada wild horses for a contraceptive study. Nutrition there is poor under the best of conditions, but the extreme cold had particularly sapped these animals. Although the stallions were in fair shape, and the nonlactating mares didn't look bad either, the lactating mares were in terrible condition. When we had finished determining the ages of the animals, we found very few middle- and old-aged mares. The drain of lactation, poor nutrition, and a frigid winter conspired to kill the unfortunate mares.

One must be careful not to generalize from just one situation. In the western part of Nevada, mortality rates are higher among stallions. Among these Granite Range wild horses, males outnumber females at birth by

1.11 to 1.0; but among adult animals, females outnumber males by 1.5 to 1.0. With that region's better food resources, even the lactating mares apparently make it through tough winters. Although the cause of the Granite Ridge stallions' high mortality rate is unknown, there is some speculation their deaths may be related to injuries suffered while fighting.

Another great killer among wild horses is drought, and nowhere can a better example be found than in central Australia. When severe droughts come along, and that happens with great regularity on that stark continent, wild horses die by the tens of thousands. On one occasion, I walked across a few miles of the outback north of Alice Springs —the ground was littered with the bleaching bones of wild horses. It was almost impossible to walk a hundred meters without finding another skeleton. These animals died in large numbers when the water disappeared, and the carnage is a terrible thing to see.

As the water sources dry up, they actually become traps for the horses. Water turns to mud, and then the mud thickens to the point where the horses become mired and unable to move. First they exhaust themselves floundering in the muck. Finally, like the animals in the deep Pryor Mountain snows, they simply lie down and die.

Diseases take wild horses, too, but we do not know very much about this subject. The carcasses of wild horses that die in remote areas are seldom discovered when fresh enough to ascertain a cause of death. Horses living in tropical areas face more peril from diseases than those living in dryer and colder climates, largely because of the greater number of insects. During the late summers of 1989 and 1990, almost 40 wild horses died on Assateague Island from Eastern Equine Encephalitis (EEE). This viral disease attacks the nervous system of horses and humans and is usually fatal in both. Brought to the island by a variety of birds, the primary carrier on Assateague is thought to be the glossy ibis. The virus is transmitted from the birds to the horses by mosquitoes. It was hardly surprising that those two summers were among the worst in the island's recent history for these sucking insects. The disease is probably always present there, but the statistical probability of contracting the disease increases with the number of mosquitoes. Infected horses slowly lose control of their muscles, develop tremors, and then die. The weakest horses, the lactating mares and old harem stallions, died most frequently.

One young bachelor stallion, an unmarked bay about eight years old, contracted the disease on Assateague Island in late summer 1990. He quickly developed the clinical symptoms, lost a good deal of motor control, and staggered about for several weeks. We expected him to die along with the other infected horses, but somehow he hung on, and within a month he regained some muscle control. Six months later, only a slightly abnormal gait in his hind legs betrayed his bout with this deadly virus. Surviving this disease is extremely rare. With his survival, the stallion's behavior became quite erratic and he was quickly dubbed "Psycho" by the researchers and park rangers. Within a year, Psycho acquired the famed Bayside mares and today is a gentle, intelligent, and successful harem stallion.

Lyme disease may kill some of the island's wild horses, but we really do not have any solid information about the frequency or the effects of this disease in these animals. It can be symptomatic in horses, and though we occasionally find a horse dead for unexplained reasons, we cannot say for certain that Lyme disease was the cause. The disease is transmitted by a bacterium carried by the deer tick. Most deer on Assateague Island are infected, but the extent of the disease in wild horses remains a mystery. Wild horses are also susceptible to various fevers and colds, distemper, colic, and mange, but just how these diseases affect mortality in wild horses is not known.

Neonatal death—death within hours or days of birth—is probably a significant form of mortality among wild horses, but its extent is unknown for all wild horse populations. Our first indication of a large number of foals dying soon after birth came from extensive observation during the foaling season. A mare would appear with her foal, and a few days later the foal would be gone. Unless we had been there and witnessed the foal, we would have had no knowledge of the loss.

*A major cause of mortality among barrier island horses is equine encephalitis,
a fatal disease brought to the island by a variety of birds and transmitted to
horses by mosquitoes.*

Foal mortality is high among wild horses. Mares will sometimes abandon foals, some are accidentally killed during fights between stallions, and a variety of diseases claims the lives of young horses during their first year.

A new technique for studying reproduction in free-roaming horses has recently given us a better look at neonatal mortality. Urine samples can be collected from the soil after a mare urinates, and the urine can be separated from the soil and analyzed for reproductive hormones. The same thing can be accomplished with fresh fecal samples. In both cases we can diagnose pregnancy with unerring accuracy without ever having touched the animals. Since fetal loss is rare at very late stages of pregnancy, neonatal loss can be determined by comparing early spring pregnancy rates with foaling rates. A mare determined to be pregnant in March who is without a foal in July probably lost that foal sometime after birth. Foal mortality—measured from birth to age one year—was estimated to be as high as 20% to 25% among all North American wild horses. Estimates of foal mortality for individual herds include 10% to 15% for horses in the Pine Nuts area of Nevada; 2% to 33% for the Pah Rah Mustang Area, northeast of Sparks, Nevada; and 7% to 10% for the Granite Range of Nevada.

The causes of death among foals are also poorly understood but probably have a great deal to do with congenital problems. Most foals succumb to general weaknesses at birth or to severe winter weather. Some foals separated from their mothers cannot find their way back. Others are abandoned by their mothers, are accidentally killed while other horses are fighting, or become helplessly mired in mud holes.

Predation is a natural control on many species of wildlife. Wolves eat caribou, bears eat moose calves, mountain lions eat deer, coyotes eat everything, and everything eats rabbits. Among large mammals, wolves, wild dogs, big cats, and bears are the primary predators; but today there are few areas left in the world outside of Africa where predators exist in sufficiently large numbers to have an effect upon populations of large ungulates. This is particularly true with wild horses. For the most part, wild horses either share their range with, or live very near, domestic livestock. Since the owners of that livestock long ago eliminated any predator large enough to kill their sheep or cattle, wild horses sharing that range also face very few predators. In many parts of North America, wolves were eradicated almost before the twentieth century, and bears have been driven into heavily forested areas. In recent years there has been a resurgence of mountain lions throughout the western United States, but these too are persecuted if they venture near livestock. Even if predators were abundant, few would be brave (or crazy) enough to attack a wild horse. Because the wild horse has only recently returned to a true wild state, and because this return coincided with systematic removal of predators, we have very little knowledge of predators' impacts on horses. We can examine the impact of hyenas, lions, leopards, and wild dogs on zebras of Africa and try to extrapolate to wild horses, but parallels and generalizations would probably be risky.

I do not believe that bears, where they do share range with wild horses, play any role at all in predation. Wild horses grazing in the Pryor Mountains within 100 meters of a black bear display little alarm or obvious concern. It is worth noting that the bears didn't pay much attention to the horses, either. In Australia, where wild horses share their range with the dingo, there is no evidence for predation. Dingoes are just not large enough to

(above) There are few predators that have a serious effect on wild horse populations in North America. Historically, wolves were a successful predator of horses, but today there are too few to have any effect on horse mortality.
(right) On the Montgomery Pass Wild Horse Territory near Bishop, California, mountain lions do have a serious impact on the mortality of foals. This is one of the few wild horse herds in North America where predation plays a role.

take on the flaying hooves of a band of wild horses. Although historical accounts indicate that wolves had a significant impact on horses, the wolf has been driven from the wild horses' range. Still, there are some interesting behaviors displayed by wild horses that suggest there is an ancient conflict between the two species.

The northern eight miles of Assateague Island are off limits to vehicles, requiring human visitors to walk a great distance or arrive by boat. Some tourists landing by boat bring their pet dogs—which is in violation of National Park Service regulations—and permit the animals to roam freely. On several occasions I have seen the horses mount a deliberate and concerted effort to attack the dogs, even though they may pose little threat. A long evolutionary memory may be at work in the horse brain.

On one occasion I witnessed an event that speaks to the intelligence of the horse and its relationship to the canine family. On the north end of Assateague lives a small bay mare with a single white stocking. We are not sure of her age, but she is at least eight years old. One day her band was grazing on the new grass of a tidal marsh pasture, one side of which was bordered by much taller grass. Looking for a mouse, or perhaps a duck dinner, a

red fox was hunting along the edge. The bay mare noticed the fox and watched it intently from a distance. The mare then lowered her head and walked slowly in the direction of the fox, pretending to be grazing. Continuing her ploy, she ambled to within 50 yards of the fox, stopping and staring to check on the little canine's position.

Continuing her charade, the horse moved ever nearer, while the fox, oblivious to her, went about its business of hunting. When the mare had approached within 30 yards, she suddenly charged the fox with malice, pounding after it at full speed. Only a quick response by the fox and some thick brush saved its hide. I have been careful over the years not to anthropomorphize and attribute human attributes to wild animals, but this was a clear case of planned deception by the mare and indicates a degree of thought and planning that surprised even me. It also was one more example of the wild horse's hostile attitude regarding canids.

The one case of successful predation of wild horses on a significant scale involves a herd living on the Montgomery Pass Wild Horse Territory on the California-Nevada border. My colleague in wild horse research for the past 22 years, Dr. John Turner,

A harem stallion challenges intruders, placing himself between his mares and the perceived danger.

discovered an interesting interaction between these horses and mountain lions. In this mountainous horse range, numerous lions prey mostly on mule deer. With the coming of spring and the foaling season, the lions switch to foals as prey. Once the foaling season is over, they return to a diet of mule deer again. The phenomenon of a predator switching prey in season is well documented. This, however, is the only incidence I know of in which wild horses become the prey. The lions do not appear to bother adult horses, but the extremely low growth rate of this particular wild horse herd attests to the impact of predation. The general absence of predators in the world of the wild horse further explains their success as a wild species.

Fighting among males results in some mortality but certainly not to a significant degree. Extensive fighting between stallions results in a lot of injuries, even occasional broken bones, but rarely deaths. The change in female-to-male ratios between young wild horses and adults in the Granite Range of Nevada, where stallion mortality is higher than mare mortality, has been attributed to fighting and the resulting wounds. Stallion mortality, however, does little to limit populations. On other wild horse ranges, while fights produce some impressive injuries, there has been no documentation of significant numbers of deaths. Fighting stallions will sometimes carry the fight right into a harem band and, on occasion, foals will suffer mortal injuries from one of the combatants.

In 1992, the Assateague band stallion N9H engaged a young stallion in a ferocious brawl. During this particularly violent fight, N9H suffered a serious wound to one of his front legs and hooves. When I saw him limp away from his band to lie still in the brush, I though he was finished. Yet a week after he disappeared he was back on his feet, even though a piece of bone protruded from the wound on his foot. I still wasn't optimistic about his chances, but he again proved me wrong. Within six months N9H had regained full charge of his band and today shows little sign of his injury.

Like other wild animals, wild horses die in collisions with vehicles. Some North American wild horses die at the hand of man, albeit illegally. In Nevada, significant numbers of horses have been shot by those who oppose their existence on public lands. In Australia, attempts at population control are carried out with the gun.

Thousands of wild horses are shot from airplanes and helicopters by government employees.

Wild horses are not immune to natural disasters. While the island horses have dealt successfully with hurricanes for hundreds of years, a freak storm that struck Assateague Island in January 1992 claimed the lives of a dozen horses. The storm hit just as dawn was breaking. Something that can only be described as a small tidal wave swept across the island's north end, carrying 12 horses to their deaths. About six or seven, because they may have been on high ground, somehow survived. The animals that were killed were swept entirely across the island. Some were found lodged in trees, and others were washed across the entire bay, their bodies found on the mainland several miles away. These incidents, although rare, contribute to the mortality rate.

Interestingly, more is known about the causes of mortality among zebras than among wild horses; perhaps—but not necessarily—there are lessons to be learned. In zebras, injuries are the most common cause of death among adults. Broken legs and severed tendons as a result of fights are common. Dental abnormalities are common among zebras but most do not cause serious health problems. Severe malocclusions of teeth—a poor alignment of upper and lower teeth—sometimes afflicts zebras and causes poor digestion, which leads to higher rates of mortality. Although I have seen one such case among the Pryor Mountain horses, there is no evidence that this is a significant cause of mortality among wild horses. Wild zebras also carry a host of parasites, including various species of ticks, worms, and insect larvae, but there is little evidence that these cause much in the way of mortality. Wild horses also carry many insect parasites, but other than equine encephalitis and perhaps some occasional Lyme disease, the consequences are not serious. Infectious diseases also appear rare among wild horses, but since we know so little about this aspect, further research is clearly needed.

Mortality among wild horses occurs from a wide variety of causes, including extreme climatic conditions, poor environmental conditions, disease, predation, and accidents. However, the overall low mortality rates of wild horses attests to the ruggedness and fitness of this species and clearly is a major cause for the unusually high growth rates among wild horse populations.

THE FUTURE OF THE WILD HORSE

"*God forbid that I should go to any heaven in which there were no horses.*"

Robert Bontaine Cunningham-Graham
In a letter to Theodore Roosevelt, 1917

e've taken a brief glimpse at the ancient history of the wild horse and a snapshot of the wild horse as it exists today, and we've learned a bit of its natural history. But what of the future of the wild horse? Will it survive as a wild species? If so, in what numbers and where? What are the rationales for protecting the species?

Like so many other subjects, the future of the wild horse is linked to the past. The great North American herds of the 1700s and 1800s, numbering in the millions, were significantly reduced during the latter half of the nineteenth century. Farming and domestic livestock replaced horses, forcing them into some of the most inhospitable retreats on the continent. Fences and guns prevented them from returning to the plains. In many respects wild horses suffered much the same fate as their western American Indian companions who were forced from their grassland homes of choice into deserts, badlands, and mountains.

Despite their forced retreat into North America's badlands, wild horses still had some value to humans. Prior to the arrival of the tractor, horses were needed for farming, pulling plows and wagons, and before the appearance of the internal combustion engine and cars, horses were still the major form of transportation. While horse breeding operations produced some of the needed animals, wild horses were gathered, domesticated, and used to drive the engines of human productivity. Wars produced an even greater demand for wild horses. During the South African Boer War of 1899-1902, and later during World War I, tens of thousands of wild horses were captured and sent off to war, to carry soldiers and pull wagons and guns. They served by the thousands, and they died by the thousands.

But with the coming of the tractor, the truck, and the car, the demand for horses declined dramatically. This decline in demand occurred simultaneously with the release of large numbers of domestic horses during the Great Depression—horses that rapidly reverted to a wild state. The human capacity for finding a use for something is almost unlimited and it was not long before the pet food industry discovered wild horses as a cheap source of meat. By the middle of this century the "mustanging" business was widespread throughout the western United States. Each year thousands of wild horses were captured and sent off to pet food plants throughout the Midwest. The wild horse became a commodity worth 14 cents a pound. Ultimately, and ironically, the practice of mustanging would work on behalf of wild horses.

It was not mustanging *per se* that led to the salvation of wild horses, but rather the excesses associated with roundups, or horse gathers, as some like to refer to them. In short, the practices used to gather and transport the horses were incredibly inhumane. Horses would be chased for miles—often in sweltering temperatures—by men on horseback, in vehicles, and even in airplanes. Those horses that survived were corralled, often for days, without shelter, food, or water. Where there were no corrals, wranglers would tie a rope from the horse's neck to an old truck tire. Even though a horse could drag the tire a bit, this "anchor" kept the animal from wandering any distance.

The wild horse no longer has commercial value and cannot be hunted. If we are to appreciate this animal, we must do so primarily for what it does for our spirit.

Conditions deteriorated even more once the horses were loaded into stock trucks. Crammed beyond capacity into metal trailers, the horses were driven great distances in intense heat or bitter cold. Without food or water, few animals survived the trip. Some might argue that since the horses' fate at the end of the trip was slaughter anyway, it made no difference if the animals died along the way. Such an argument falls short of that which we attribute to the minds of civilized people and does not deserve the dignity of a response.

In the 1950s Mrs. Velma Johnson, of Reno, Nevada, witnessed just such a scene as I have described. Outraged at the treatment of the horses, she began a life's mission to put an end to mustanging. Once the general public became aware of the terrible acts visited upon wild horses, the plight of these animals became known by the United States Congress. Behind the leadership of Mrs. Johnson, or Wild Horse Annie, as she was more commonly known, increasing public pressure led Congress to pass legislation in 1959 prohibiting the gathering, chasing, or harassing of horses with motorized vehicles or airplanes. However, wild horses could still be captured or even killed under state laws. Mrs. Johnson continued to pressure Congress. Hundreds of thousands of letters, telegrams, and phone calls on behalf of the humane treatment of wild horses flooded Congress during the 1960s. This public outcry led directly to the passage on December 12, 1971 of Public Law 92-195, the Wild Horse and Burro Act. This law made all wild horses living on public lands in the United States the property of the government, providing almost complete protection to wild horses under the "management" of the Bureau of Land Management (BLM), the National Park Service (NPS), and the U.S. Forest Service (USFS). Put another way, the Wild Horse and Burro Act cast the U.S. government into the role of the world's largest horse breeding operation.

It took only a few years after the passage of this legislation for these agencies to realize just how remarkable the reproductive capacity of wild horses was. Soon the government was caught foursquare between those who wanted wild horses on our public lands and those who felt the horses were unneeded competition for livestock and other species of consumable wildlife. Mrs. Johnson died not too many years after the passage of the Wild Horse and Burro Act. Despite lingering issues regarding America's wild horses, Mrs. Johnson's legacy of increased public awareness and more humane treatment of the nation's wild horses speaks eloquently of her untiring efforts.

At the time of the passage of the Wild Horse and Burro Act there were an estimated 17,000 wild horses living on public lands. That number, however, was merely a good guess, and its accuracy has been a point of debate for many years. Regardless of the accuracy of this number, by 1980 there were somewhere between 65,000 and 80,000 wild horses. This dramatic population increase in turn led to three major public camps, each with their own particular concerns. The most rabid wild horse advocates felt the numbers were purposely inflated by the government to provide an excuse for removal of horses, which they opposed. Another group of horse advocates were less nervous about the estimated numbers and rates of increases of wild horses, and they understood that some form of control needed to be applied to the herds. However, they were divided on how best to reduce the size of the horse herds. The third group consisted largely of agricultural users of public lands and wildlife advocates who viewed the wild horse as a threat to other species. For the most part they wanted large reductions in the number of wild horses and they didn't particularly care how the reductions occurred.

Simple destruction of the horses was not possible. Both the public and Congress found that solution unacceptable. Faced with a lack of alternatives, Congress authorized the removal and adoption of "excess" horses, and the now famous Adopt-A-Horse program was born. In 1973, 23 wild horses were removed from the Pryor Mountain Wild Horse refuge in Montana and adopted by private owners. In 1974 a similar program was initiated in Oregon. Although this program grew rapidly, it wasn't without complications. While this relatively humane approach to controlling wild horse populations was generally acceptable, two major problems emerged almost immediately.

The Bureau of Land Management attempts to control populations by gathering the horses and transferring them to private individuals through the Adopt-A-Horse program.

If we say wild horses have overpopulated, what exactly do we mean? What constitutes "excess" horses? We can use a wildlife biologist's definition and say that they are overpopulated if they have overused their ranges and can't support themselves in a healthy manner. Or, since most of these horses must share their range with domestic livestock, we can define overpopulation as too many horses using grass and water that might otherwise be used by sheep or cattle. From the limited viewpoint of a reproductive biologist, I might view the horses as overpopulated if their high population density caused decreased reproductive rates. A pathologist might declare the horses to be overpopulated if density-induced stress caused mortal or debilitating diseases. Perhaps a behavioral biologist might declare horses to be overpopulated when high densities caused significant behavioral changes among the animals. Thus, the very first ecological problem—overpopulation—was in reality either a policy problem or a problem of perception.

The second problem came with the actual implementation and costs of Adopt-A-Horse. Developing humane capture methods took time and created controversy. The costs for capture, selecting recipients, and

distributing animals were as high as $1,000 per animal and averaged close to $600. The adoption fee of $125 per horse did little to offset these costs and the adoption program began to cost the government millions. By 1992, an estimated $121 million had been spent on the management of America's wild horses. The Wild Horse and Burro Act was amended twice in the 1970s to facilitate capture by permitting the use of aircraft for gathering animals and trucks for transporting them. But by the 1980s it was obvious that it simply wasn't possible to remove and adopt enough horses to control the populations. The market for these horses grew saturated. Because animals from certain horse ranges—such as the Pryor Mountains, Oregon's Kiger Plateau, and Virginia's Chincoteague National Wildlife—are perceived as unique, they always sold readily. But other larger ranges could not get rid of their tenants as easily. The estimated 9,000 to 11,000 adoptions per year that budgets, the market, and the constraints of humane treatment would allow turned out to be too low to control a population of 50,000 to 60,000 wild horses.

The public's adoption preferences resulted in yet another problem. Most preferred young females and

Most people want to adopt young mares and foals, probably because they are easier to train. Removing these young animals is often self-defeating because the older mares that remain behind reproduce at faster rates as a result.

only 11% would adopt a stallion. This spawned two undesirable effects. First, large numbers of unadoptable horses accumulated in the government corrals, forcing the government to care for and feed thousands of captive animals. By 1986 the costs for maintaining these animals had reached $7 million per year. The second undesirable effect resulted from the removal of young females. Most were less than two years old and were still nursing. When they were removed, their mothers stopped lactating, started ovulating, got pregnant, and produced new foals. With textbook precision, the wild horses left behind on the ranges reproduced at higher-than-ever rates. By the late 1980s, the government had spent millions of dollars removing, adopting, and maintaining thousands of wild horses, and still there were as many as 50,000 left in the wild.

In Australia, where estimates of wild horse numbers ran as high as 300,000 to 600,000, the issues were much simpler. There were too many horses. They were either gathered and sold or shot from airplanes. While not popular with the public, the absence of protective legislation similar to the Wild Horse and Burro Act allows the controversy to continue "down under." The government continues to shoot wild horses or send them off to rendering plants, and a rapidly growing Australian animal welfare community continues to wage a verbal and legal war against their government.

The issues haven't changed much since the Wild Horse and Burro Act was passed. Conflict with livestock growers over grazing resources, competition with other wildlife, and degradation of habitat continue to be the rallying points for the opponents of wild horses. And today, in 1994, the questions are still about the same. Are there too many horses? Should the populations be reduced? By what method and by how much should they be reduced? Those who argue on behalf of these animals do so because of the wild horses' special place in the history of the United States, but their arguments have expanded to include other considerations as well. There are those who now argue that America's wild horses can provide us with important information about the evolution of the horse—and even about the biology of domestic horses. Others have become more conscious that public lands where wild horses live belong to everyone and that these lands are not the exclusive domain of ranchers. Consequently, people from all over the United States now feel they have a stake in wild horses.

How valid are the arguments against the wild horse? At the outset, let us agree that wild horses need some form of population control here in North America. The remarkable reproductive capacity of the animals and

their adaptability make it clear that, left unmanaged, they are capable of destroying their ranges and doing harm to themselves in the process. That issue was settled and agreed upon by both the opponents and advocates of wild horses in 1982. Until that time, most advocates were still uneasy about wild horse population estimates and whether any control at all was necessary. But in a landmark meeting of animal protection societies in Washington, D.C., in May 1982, there was common agreement that some form of control had to be applied. Then new dimensions of the problem emerged.

Were wild horses guilty as accused for doing all the damage to natural resources, or did domestic livestock have an impact also? Which creatures were doing the most damage? This question seems particularly important when it is pointed out that cattle, sheep, and goats outnumber wild horses on public lands by 4.5 to 1. With unusual candor, the Chief of the Division of Wild Horses for the BLM stated in 1986 that there was no evidence that the impact of wild horses was more severe than that of other wildlife or domestic livestock.

But the wild horse controversy lives on anyway. Most of the public lands upon which they live are managed under the "multiple use" concept. Grazing, mining, logging, and recreation are all permitted in various degrees, and the wild horse resides in the middle of all this. A typical conflict is the one that threatens to reduce the number of Pryor Mountain horses in the 1990s. A growing population of reintroduced bighorn sheep share the range with these horses. As desires to expand sheep hunting increase, so have calls prompting a reduction in the size of the wild horse herd. Those who call for such a reduction on these grounds forget that the Pryor Mountain National Wild Horse Refuge was created by Congress for wild horses, and not for bighorn sheep, or elk, or mule deer. *For wild horses.* The horses are maintained at or about 130 animals and they have always shared the range with sheep, elk, and deer. There are those who ask, and I am among them, why must the horse population be reduced to make room for more sheep? Why can't sheep populations be reduced to permit the established number of 130 horses? The answer is central to the dilemma of the wild horse.

The larger issue, however, remains the perceived conflict between horses and domestic livestock. I say perceived, because portraying wild horses as causing a problem may be inaccurate. Wild horses certainly do not threaten the livestock industry, since only about 2% of the entire U.S. cattle herd grazes on public lands.

(below) Pounding hooves resound and dust swirls about a band of horses as they race across the prairie. (right) A king of the badlands patrols his home range. Such a magnificent scene as this is the goal of all who value wild horses.

If there is truly a need to reduce wild horses because of damage to the resource—grass in this case—then equal reductions should occur among domestic livestock on these same lands. It is unlikely that this conflict will soon disappear, but new solutions are on the horizon.

Earlier we examined the two controls placed on wildlife populations: mortality control and reproductive success. Natural mortality control is not occurring, and removal has not kept pace with reproduction. That leaves only fertility control. Natural fertility control, where reproductive success slows or stops because of increased population densities, is not occurring among most wild horses. They have not yet reached maximum population densities at which this natural control will occur. There are, however, artificial forms of fertility control. The concept at first sounds bizarre but is coming of age with regard to wildlife control. In the early 1970s, research was started to seek ways to reduce sperm counts among wild stallions. Although the research later proved pharmacologically successful, stallions had to be captured and injected with huge doses of hormonal drugs, making the technique impractical to apply. Similar research with hormonal implants aimed at controlling reproduction in mares was also pharmacologically successful, but some members of the public felt the stress to the horses caused by capture and field surgery was unacceptable.

In 1988 a breakthrough occurred in fertility control research with the Assateague wild horses. Instead of administering a hormonal drug, which necessitated a "hands on" approach, mares were inoculated with a vaccine that made them immune to their own eggs. The vaccine could be given remotely with an injection delivered by small darts, eliminating the handling of horses. It was highly effective and better than 95% of treated mares failed to produce foals. The vaccine's contraceptive effects were reversible, and it didn't alter the social structure or behaviors of the population. Production of the vaccine was relatively inexpensive, and the vaccine wouldn't pass through the food chain if an animal died and was consumed. Today the Assateague wild horses are managed with this vaccine, ending the days of capture and removal.

The BLM is currently conducting large scale trials with the same vaccine in Nevada. In this case, helicopters are used to drive the wild horses into a trap, which consists of two long "fences" made of baling twine and burlap. Though they could easily run through these flimsy fences, the horses assume that they are solid and are funneled toward portable corrals. A "Judas" mare helps. This is a domestic mare trained to stand at the entrance of the trap, and when the wild horses enter the open end, she runs down into the corrals. The wild horses, seeing the Judas mare running ahead of them, apparently believe she is just another wild mare and that she knows what she is doing, so they follow her into the trap. After that, the mares are herded through a chute and inoculated by hand. As of 1994, this research and its application to large numbers of wild horses is still in its early stages, but the results thus far have been promising and suggest that a publicly acceptable solution to controlling populations may be near.

The future of the wild horse is dependent upon a number of factors. First, the future for this species will undoubtedly differ from continent to continent and country to country, and the largest single factor controlling the fate of wild horses anywhere will be public opinion. It is unlikely that Australian or New Zealand wild horses will ever achieve the popularity of America's populations, and if I am correct in that assumption, they will continue to be destroyed for many years to come. Having painted that gloomy picture, it is also unlikely that wild horses will disappear from Australia. There are simply too many and the continent is too vast. In America, however, the wild horse will survive and even thrive, probably at a population level of about 40,000 animals.

The keys to survival in the United States are the existing protective legislation and the public's love affair with wild horses. For over 20 years there have been calls for the repeal of the Wild Horse and Burro Act by opponents of wild horses, but it is extremely unlikely that Congress will even consider such an act. Passage of animal

(below) On some coastal barrier islands, wild horses share their home ranges with sika deer. These small deer are relatives of the elk and native to Taiwan and Japan. There is little competition between the sika deer and horses.
(right) Pronghorn antelope and horses evolved together on the western prairies. The horse has returned home after a long absence and fits well into its former ecological niche.

protection legislation is often difficult, but history has shown us that repeal of these laws is even more difficult. The wild horses' future is further assured by the public's perception of the wild horse as one of only a few remaining symbols of the romance of the Old West.

Perhaps no single species of wildlife evokes the emotions of the public to a greater degree than the wild horse. The reasons for these reactions are not entirely clear and they may be tied to the confused and twisted history of *Equus caballus*, the modern horse. Whatever the causes, the public's view of this spectacular animal is as diverse as the ranges they inhabit. To the wildlife purists, the wild horse is not even considered a legitimate claimant to the title of wildlife. The thoroughbred breeder and other enthusiasts of the domestic horse world see only ugly, ill-proportioned "jugheads" that have let their genes go to seed, so to speak. Those with an appreciation for history see an animal that changed the very destiny of man here and abroad. Those who are especially fond of U.S. western history see the horses as a legacy left by our forebears, both native and immigrant. The western rancher sometimes sees only a ward of the state that is eating grass that might better go to his cattle or sheep. Finally, members of Congress see the wild horse as a fact of life that generates a great deal of their mail and a species that can consume federal dollars on the same scale they can consume grass.

Somewhere in these diverse views lies the true nature of the wild horse. This is an animal that evolved in North America, leaving and returning to the continent several times over the past 60 million years, only to mysteri-ously disappear for good about 12,000 years ago. With the aid of man, the animals returned almost 500 years ago, reestablishing themselves on the land where they evolved. During the brief time it has been "home," the horse was the engine that drove the exploration of the continent, it was central to the creation of an entire new Native American horse culture on the Great Plains, and then it finally took leave of man's control to establish itself as one of nature's most successful wild species. This history, and the dual role of this animal as both a companion animal and a wildlife species, makes the wild horse unique. It also brings to focus the horse's major problem.

The elk is a revered species on our continent, but I wonder how it would be perceived if it was not a game animal. This species provides recreation for those who hunt it and huge amounts of revenue for the states in which they live. The same can be said of most other large species of ungulates in North America, such as the white-tailed deer, the mule deer, antelope, moose, and bighorn sheep, just to name a few. But how would these same species be perceived and embraced by the public if they could not be hunted and if they did not generate revenue? Worse, what if they cost the taxpayer large sums of money to have around? Would we still love them and protect them?

Among the large hoofed animals of our continent, the wild horse stands alone as a species without value as a game animal and one that does not generate revenue for the states in which it lives. It is a noncommercial, nongame animal that lives its life in solitude. It asks nothing from man and it gets very little.

Humans have persecuted the species and they have protected it, too, but most of us really know very little about these mysterious creatures as they exist today. In the meadows of the Pryor Mountains, or the swamps of Assateague Island, I sometimes come across those rare adventurous people who are fascinated by these magnificent animals. I'm constantly amazed at how little they know of the wild horses' basic natural history or their wonderful social order. And, I am always rewarded by their delight and wonderment once they have learned even a few basic facts.

But now we come to the value of the wild horse, and like everything else in its history, this value is unique on our continent. If we are to appreciate these animals at all, we must appreciate them simply because of their aesthetic value as wild creatures. They have no other important human value associated with large wildlife species—the Medicine Dog has only value to the spirit. A glimpse of a wild horse has no promise of meat, of the thrill of the hunt, of license sales, or of market values. This glimpse offers only whatever value can be obtained from the view itself.

I have stood upon the rock outcrops of the high Pryor Mountains, the holy lands of the Crow Indians, watching grulla and buckskin mares with their foals and their black stallion grazing on alpine meadows as they have done for 200 years, framed by the awesome Beartooth Mountains to the west. I watched bands of wild horses run free across the sage-covered hills of Challis, Idaho, leaving plumes of dust in their wake. In the billabongs of Australia's Northern Territories I watched tough sorrels and chestnuts, on their way to precious water, cautiously file their way through the spinifex plants and bird-filled eucalyptus trees. Watching a young mare in the Book Cliffs of Utah emerge with a wobbly new foal, after their days of secret hiding, makes me giddy and lighthearted for days. To see a stallion and a mare affectionately groom each other, amid the man-height sagebrush of Wyoming's silent Red Desert, fills me with awe. And, if there is anything more beautiful on this earth than standing alone in an Assateague marsh in a cold March sunset, watching a band of brown and white pintos graze peacefully while snow geese glide overhead and sika deer gracefully prance through on their way to some favorite feeding place, I want to discover it before my own journey is finished. I am richer, beyond description, because of these events.

And *that* is the value of the wild horse.